A SPECIAL PLACE IN HELL...

Healing An Epidemic of Unhappy Women

April Churchill

Copyright 2008 by April Churchill

ISBN: 978-0-615-26212-3

healinganepidemic@gmail.com
Find this book at www.lulu.com

"There is a special place in hell
for women
who don't help other women."

~Madeleine K. Albright
Former United States Secretary of State and
United States Ambassador to the UN

ACKNOWLEDGMENTS

My small words can only express so much.
To Mom, Dad, Danielle and Kim.
Thank you for your patience, your unconditional love and forgiveness,
and for never giving up.

And especially to Anthony.
Thank you for being exactly who you are and for making my life,
and this world,
a much better place.
All my love.

CONTENTS

Page

	Author's Note	*3*
	Introduction	*9*
1:	**An Unrealistic Ideal of Perfection**	*11*
2:	**Choose Happiness**	*17*
3:	**The Martyr**	*25*
4:	**The Appeaser**	*43*
5:	**The I Just Can't Win**	*61*
6:	**The Brooder**	*77*
7:	**The Bitch**	*93*
8:	**The One Upper**	*111*
9:	**The Hypochondriac**	*127*
10:	**The Happy One**	*145*
	Reference	*155*

AUTHOR'S NOTE

I was determined to write <u>A Special Place In Hell...Healing An Epidemic of Unhappy Women</u>, because I am *deeply* concerned about the state of our world's mothers, daughters, sisters and wives. A vast number of these extraordinary women are sincerely happy with their lives and are making a positive impact in the lives of those they touch, but there are also a great number of these women, who have the capability and influence to create so much good and progress, who are needlessly suffering from a devastating epidemic.

Today, depression is the second leading cause of disability among women, ages 15-44, and the fourth leading contributor to the global burden of disease. By 2020, if nothing is done to decelerate the current rate of depression, it will be the second leading cause of disability for all ages, and both sexes, world wide.[1] **The second leading cause of disability in the world!** Our unresolved turmoil is literally leaving us disabled and, inevitably, emotionally disabled women lead to emotionally disabled lives, relationships, families, children, workplaces and communities.

These increasing numbers are staggering. If we continue to neglect the importance of maintaining our mental, emotional and physical health we will only be left with continued despair; leading us down a disconnected path to tragedy. The good news, however, is *our future doesn't have to unfold this way*.

Throughout my lifetime I have been surrounded by, quite simply, some absolutely amazing women; my mother, sisters, grandmothers, great-grandmothers, aunts, in-laws, mentors, friendships (some wonderful, others turbulent) and my many professional pursuits have always provided me with an abundant source of inspiration. I am fortunate to have been surrounded by strong passionate women but, at times, within these relationships, what I have continued to witness both fascinates and disturbs me: instead of living lives that are full and connected, we -all too often- become disillusioned with our purpose, our place and our extraordinary influence. We can be *terribly* critical of each other and even more critical of ourselves! Together, as women, we could be a powerful force of compassion and strength but sadly, we tend to be our own worst enemy.

As individuals, when we are happy with who we are and our place in this world, we motivate and support each other, regardless of our differences. We create positivity and connectedness within our own lives and in the lives of those with whom we interact, because when we are healthy and *feel* good we *are* good, to ourselves and to each other! Residing in a happy and healthy existence allows us to become, and project, an unstoppable positive force of motivation and connectedness. Basically, when we are happy this world is a much better place.

However, when we are *unhappy* as individuals, when we become fixated on what we think *isn't* good in our lives, a different kind of force is awakened: one that is both negative and horribly destructive. When we are discontent in who we are, we become quick to turn against one another and offer no refrain from tearing other women apart. We become emotionally isolated, push others away and become a catalyst for disrespect and criticism. Our unsettled souls create an imbalance, not just in our personal lives but also in the lives of everyone who is a part of our existence.

When we are unhappy and refuse to address the cause of our personal unsettledness, discontentment is what we continue to feel, what we continue to give and what we continue to receive.

Author's Note

There are a number of factors that contribute to feelings of unhappiness and, when ignored, can possibly lead to a state of depression. Biological, genetic, environmental and emotional factors (just to name a few) can all have a dramatic impact on our daily lives, and although depression is <u>very</u> real and each of these factors are certainly legitimate, *they do not have to debilitate us.*

First and foremost, I am not an expert on emotional disorders nor depression, but after years of being lost in my own darkness, battling and conquering addiction, being diagnosed and treated for severe depression, surviving life experiences of trial and error and error, deep loss, quiet observation, silent contemplation and a lot of good therapy, have I realized how accessible a life of happiness really is. I have fought it, shunned it, craved it and finally embraced it. The answer is simple...

You choose to be happy.

Happiness isn't about perfection,
it isn't about monetary gain
and it isn't about
an ultimate finish line that has to be reached.
Happiness is about choice.

The simple choices you make every day determine your happiness:

Your personal well-being affects how you view yourself, your life and the people in it.
Your willingness to participate in a meaningful level of connectedness, determines the kind of relationships you will develop.

Acknowledging your personal weakness, provides you with the opportunity to conquer debilitating insecurities.
Your choices determine your acceptance of living a life that is full, or one that is empty.

The process really is that simple, and regardless of the type of woman you choose to be -a happy or unhappy one- you will assuredly affect those who surround you: for the good and for the bad. Because as a woman, *you affect everyone*.

You have the extraordinary power to create peace, or hostility, within all of your relationships and, inescapably, what you choose to create will be what you receive in return.

You have so much control over your happiness!

This book is not written to categorize or judge other women. I have written it to share with you my thoughts, observations and experiences involving the power of choice and to encourage you to embrace a happy, productive way of life. If you read something familiar, or identify with the issues that routinely keep women frozen in a life of disconnectedness, get excited (and motivated) to dig to the root of when you started living this way! Because once you choose to acknowledge the cause of your unhappiness, you will give your mind, body and spirit the opportunity to find a new, healthy way to experience living; making the world a better place for you and everyone in it.

There is so much in this lifetime to be grateful for, but in order to see it you have to be willing to take a deep breath, clear your eyes and agree to open your heart. You deserve to feel inner peace not misery.

Author's Note

You are suppose to experience connectedness not separation, and you are capable of having a life that gives you the very good you choose to create! Beginning right now, the choice is yours...

    Be kind to each other and be well,
       April

INTRODUCTION

You are an integral part of an absolutely extraordinary group! There are over two billion, one hundred fourteen million, seven hundred and thirty thousand of us living on this planet. We span across the miles, live amongst different cultures, have unique perspectives on life yet all share a major commonality: ***we are women***. Each day, every single one of us wakes up and does our best to make sense of this world; we are all living and breathing at the exact same moment, some of us deeply and others just barely.

Somewhere within this massive number, a wife is about to receive the most exhilarating news of her life as another, tragically, hears her most devastating. A group of girlfriends will be overcome with laughter while, elsewhere, a mother painfully begins to grieve. A daughter will take selfishly as a grandmother loves wholeheartedly; a sister will graciously give of herself while her coworker hates with a vengeance. We are all doing *something*...

What do you contribute to this noble group?

Do you positively or negatively respond to the other 2,114,729,000+ women that make up our world's daughters, sisters and mothers: women who are heavier or thinner than you, make more or less money or have lighter or darker skin? How do you treat women who are younger or older than you, who have a higher or lesser degree of education and what about women who believe in a different religion? Do you make eye contact with those women who aren't like you? Do you offer a smile? Or do you instantly size them up and take inventory of what is "wrong" with them?

You either add strength to, or cause disintegration within, the 2.1 billion.

Which do you choose to create...

How about the relationships with the women in your family: tight-knit or unraveled? Do you consider yourselves a group of connected matriarchs who look at each other through eyes of admiration? Are you friends to one another, or do you cringe at the thought of having to spend even a second together?

Are you a happy woman...

There are so many of us that inhabit this planet. The degree to which we take care of ourselves, how we interact with each other and through the level of our personal connectedness we are *literally* "changing the world" every day, moment by moment, for the good or for the bad. Together, we can create unwavering strength and simplify the madness that so often surrounds us. We are meant to be happy and each one of us has the ability to make this life more healthy -and fulfilling- for ourselves, our family, our workplace and our community. So why would we choose to make it more complicated instead of more meaningful?

Does it really have to be this way?
Read on, you are about to find out...

Chapter 1

An Unrealistic Ideal of Perfection

1

"A woman must be...
Kind but not too kind.
Strong but not too strong.
Soft but not too soft.
Hard but not too hard.
Honest but not too honest.
Successful but not too successful.
Intelligent but not too intelligent.
Pretty but not too pretty.
Assertive but not too assertive.
Funny but not too funny.
Sexual but not too sexual.
Thin but not too thin.
Independent but not too independent.
Driven but not too driven.
Happy but not too happy.
Wise but not too wise.
The best wife.
The best lover.
The best employee.
The best mother.
The best daughter.
The best partner.
The best sister.
The best friend.
She must know when she is being too much of one thing,
And not enough of another.
And
She must be perfect."
(but not too perfect)

~April Churchill

*T*alk about pressure! It's no wonder women are often stigmatized as being "ultra-sensitive," "melodramatic" and sometimes even "a little crazy." Anyone attempting to live up to this unrealistic ideal of perfection could easily become overwhelmed, but being the determined bunch we are, we keep going. We hold it together the best way we know how, the best way we've been taught and the best way we think works. We succeed in maintaining a sense of order and balance in our lives, and relationships, but we are human: we will have moments where we fail.

Rather than simply accept that, even when we give our best, there may be a situation we won't handle, we may not always "look" just right and we may fall short of perfection, we instead end up frustrated, uptight and eventually miserable. When we are stuck in this emotional state, we tend to avoid people who are happy, mumble about our own problems and try to erase our own feelings of inadequacy by searching for deficiencies in others (usually, other women). Instead of embracing exactly what makes us unique and happily residing in our truest selves, we become consumed with unhealthy fixations. Our underlying mental, physical, and emotional discontent is what inhibits us from being open to each other and accepting of ourselves.

When we feel secure in who we are, and our place in this world, we have no room, time nor desire for criticism. Instead of feeling a nagging need to live up to unattainable expectations, we are able to focus on what *really* matters: our well-being and the well-being of those who surround us.

You are meant to be *happy*!

You have this lifetime to build, or destroy, what is good. It is *essential* that you take care of yourself, through healthy means, and address any issues that may be keeping your soul dim, your heart cold and preventing you from manifesting the goodness that is *in every single one of us*.

When you *feel* good, you *are* good; you do good things and positively contribute to the world that surrounds you, but the only person who can determine the depth and magnitude of that very goodness is: **you**.

This book is written to encourage your healthiness and to help redirect your focus inward, on your amazing intrinsic qualities! When you are healthy, and happy, you are not as susceptible to the effects of negativity and cynicism. You can more easily see the good in others and the beauty that exists in your own self, and whether you are a stay at home mom, a corporate leader, a college student or a grandmother, you are meant to be happy! *We are all meant to be happy!*

Choose to *enjoy* your life, not *endure* it, and start to find the beauty in all of the people that are a part of your life. Free up the time, and space, spent wasted on striving for perfection to strive toward becoming the healthiest version of you! Once you decide to bring positive change to your life, you will have the ability to bring that good to others; first to your family; then on to your circle of friends, your community, your city, your state, your nation and amazingly, the good will find its way back to you. The strength that is needed to change your life is already inside you! Choose to find it and start putting it to use.

Chapter 2

Choose Happiness

2

*"Our task must be to free ourselves...by widening our circle
of compassion to embrace all living creatures
and the whole of Nature in its beauty."*
~Albert Einstein

Your thoughts, the words you use, your posture, mood, tone of voice and your actions are only SOME of the factors that make you who you are. Without even consciously trying, your behavior influences every "body" you come in contact with: mentally, emotionally, physically even physiologically. What you do in your daily life, and the way you interact with others, offers balance and motivation to your world or tension and chaos. Which of these contributions are you choosing to make?

The joy you experience throughout your lifetime has a direct correlation to the way you participate in, and view, the world around you; if you find yourself in a state of unease, more often than a state of happiness, you likely jump around emotionally within each of the, soon to be explained, "seven unhealthy roles." Time and time again, you may heavily trod through the same destructive cycles, have reoccurring problems, unhealthily handle stress and experience only fleeting moments of happiness (not a pleasant way to go through life and certainly not fun). The "seven roles" are listed below and they may come across as being descriptively quite harsh, but that is simply because they **are** harsh, a harsh miserable means of existence:

The Brooder
always on the verge of a nervous breakdown, but we never know why

The Martyr
the one who, in her mind, has always had it worse than everybody else,
she can only feel peace through suffering

The Appeaser
will never speak her mind for fear of offending or upsetting,
takes care of everyone but dutifully neglects herself

The I Just Can't Win
her misery is, and always has been, everyone else's fault

The Hypochondriac
has every ailment and disease she has heard of or read about;
can't get healthy enough to live healthily

The One-Upper
impossible to have a conversation with because consists of
1) how much more she has done 2) how much more she is doing
3) how much more she will continue to do than everybody else

The Bitch:
the woman who is malicious and unpleasant and finds fault in everyone
and everything, excluding herself

<u>The Happy One:</u>
she is comfortable in her own skin, contributing and mindful
sees the good in others
who we admire and go to for advice

At different points in our lives, we are all a little of each of these women; some days we feel great and other days, we don't. We are beautifully emotional beings, and we feel to all extremes. It's our emotion that makes us so alive and our emotion that drives us to act or react, to create or destroy, to persevere or simply give up; we love and fear, rejoice and hurt, we laugh and cry, we cherish and grieve. Our lives are always enhanced by what we feel BUT there is a distinct line between simply *feeling* a particular emotion and *becoming trapped in*, and *defined* by, that emotion.

Honoring what you feel (whether it is positive or negative) and *learning* from your life experiences, and relationships, is what healthiness and happiness are all about. If you lose sight of the simple humanness in just feeling an emotion and, instead, become hyper-focused on what causes you stress, sadness, fatigue, anxiety or frustration you may find yourself entering into a world dictated solely by emotion and "tuned out" from the reality of the world that actually surrounds you. Not only will an unhealthy preoccupation, with despair and negativity, affect your physical and emotional state, but chronic depression is so toxic that it also affects the way your brain *actually* functions. When you are depressed, your brain doesn't properly work the way it is intended. It is not your natural state to always be unhappy.

If you choose to ignore the warning signs of depression or refuse to address the issues that cause your sadness, and emotional instability, you may find yourself yielding to harmful coping mechanisms in order to satiate your natural desire for happiness: emotional isolation, negative self-talk, unhealthy relationships or substance abuse. And with a broken spirit, hazy mind and chaotic emotions you may begin to accept this destructive behavior as a "normal" way of life.

When you view your life through a distorted kaleidoscope of perception, you do not allow yourself the opportunity to actually experience it in a positive healthy progression; which only leads to a disconnected, frozen way of thinking, living and being.

Personal unhappiness leads to an unhappy existence for you and everyone that is *a part* of your existence. But guess what?

Your life DOES NOT have be this way!

It is possible to live one kind of life and for there to be one type of woman: A Happy One. And throughout this book, you are going to explore different ways to conquer the restricting roles that could be preventing you from being your healthiest, happiest self.

Yes, you will have days where anything that can go wrong does, your energy level will be low and you just won't feel good, but ultimately *happiness*, not misery, can be your baseline. The process is not complicated, sugarcoated or mystical; it is simply practical. Happiness boils down to one thing: CHOICE.

1) **What** you fill your life with
2) **Who** you fill your life with
3) **How** you respond to change and unpredictability
4) And if you **choose to reside in your truest self**

Creating your own happiness, begets happiness.

That's it. It is that simple.

Your time has come to shine! Open your eyes to the issues that keep you from becoming your healthiest, truest self and surrender to the possibility of change. As individuals, we all have beautiful qualities that make us our own being. No one, NO ONE is exactly like you, nor will anyone EVER BE exactly like you. Be *your best self* and embrace what makes you unique. Focus on what is good in your life! While you are in the process take notice of other women, who are developing their own strengths, and regardless of their occupation, religion, weight, race or age *respect them for choosing to be their best selves too.*

Believe in the strength that is already inside you; begin to heal your wounds, banish your insecurities and curb your judgments. Choose to let go of the role you have been playing and redirect your focus to all that is positive, not negative, because once you begin to honestly embrace the raw love and beauty in yourself, you can begin to embrace that exact love and beauty in others. Your mind, heart and spirit will instantly become open to giving, and receiving, that which is real, pure and undeniable...

Happiness.

Chapter 3

The Martyr

3

"No one can make you feel inferior without your consent."
                                            ~Eleanor Roosevelt

*W*e know who we are...

...the women who are always suffering. Our expression is sullen and our eyes are sad, even when we smile. When asked how we are, our go-to response is always, "Oh, I'm OK." Happy moments flow through our lives on an undercurrent of despair because we know more suffering is waiting for us, right around the corner. We hold on to pain because pain is familiar; without it we feel uncomfortable, like we are missing something. Our sorrow defines us. The connection we have to other people stems from sharing our angst, and we feel closest to others in times of instability and agony. Living without chaos is a foreign concept to us and only when we are in our most fragile state, do we tap into our strength. We feel we are most loved and understood when people have sympathy for us. Our strife is felt by everyone, and after spending time with us others feel sorry for our lives, they feel unsettled and they feel absolutely drained.

You forget there is so much peace inside you waiting to be experienced, but the focus you lend to your hurting heart leaves the good to be felt humbly waiting in the wings. The time has come to heal your pain.

Life is hard, there is no question about it. You can prepare for the worst, hope for the best and wish for the most, but only one thing is for certain:

each day you are given will be ever changing.

Challenges are an inevitable part of your life. It is impossible to walk through this lifetime without experiencing sadness, pain and heartache as well as joy, excitement and triumph. You are a human being, you are meant to feel, and if you want to experience any joy in your life, you have to accept the unavoidable fact that you will, at some point, experience pain.

The good times and bad times create a kind of "dance" between the balance of emotion: you cannot know one without knowing the other. Delight and agony will appear and vanish, only to reappear again regardless of what you "want" to happen, and it's fantastic because your personal experiences, both positive and negative, are what enrich your life. They do not have to create any unwanted burden unless you decide to let them.

The dance of emotion allows you to decide, for yourself, whether you glide, fiercely stomp, slowly waltz or passionately cha-cha when faced with happiness or adversity, and the most important component of this give and take is being able to simply *stay on your feet*.

Your life is not about suffering for the right to feel good, it is about living! The way you respond to challenge, and adversity, directly affects the well of resilience you will develop throughout your lifetime: a well you will later dip into during times of uncertainty.

Your character is not measured by how much pain you have

endured or how difficult your life has been, nor is your substance based on how many battles you have fought. *How you have handled* the difficulties in your life is what matters! You will either develop healthy ways to thrive and survive or you will allow the inevitable curve balls of life to destroy you. Challenges will always exist but your self-pity and misery do not have to.

Fortify your soul by diligently working through the heavy moments in your life. Being faced with adversity it is not an indication of the end of your happiness, it is an opportunity to find your strength.

Where are you right now in spite of your trials? Have you shut down, hidden in a corner and gone numb. Or have you picked yourself up, put your shoulders back and chosen to press on? The strength you need to rise to the peaks of peace is already inside you! But it is your choice to either ignore that strength and wallow in your heaviness and despair, or to dig deep, put one foot in front of the other and lead yourself to a place of happiness. Take a moment to think about how a baby begins to walk; she certainly doesn't come out of the womb running! She always starts with a little help.

Learning how to walk is a process and usually, someone will provide their own hands -for the baby's delicate fingers to cling to- to offer her a better sense of balance. The child then uses her tiny feet to figure out some method of stabilization. Once she masters the uncertainty of finding the ground, she'll slowly start to put one foot in front of the other which, as a result, develops strength in her legs. Each leg will grow stronger, each step more solid and her confidence will continue to build. Gradually, she will let go of outside support and depend less on supplemental strength, because she will finally be creating and using her own. With a more solid step, each stride becomes longer and with longer strides, she'll make progress and cover more ground. Eventually, the child will no longer rely on outside strength to determine when, or where, she will walk. She'll be doing it on her own! The same process applies to healing your sorrow.

From your very first steps, you were not meant to walk through this lifetime alone; in facing any tragedy or turmoil, you will have moments where you will feel weak and experience circumstances that will leave you frail. You are human and in persevering through times of despair and sadness, it will not make you any less of a person to ask for, and willingly accept, a little help: someone who can "hold your hand" and offer you a sense of support and balance. Whether it is a friend, your spouse, a therapist, a parent, a religious leader, a sibling or God, whomever provides you with the encouragement to press on, graciously acknowledge their openness and accept that it is sometimes necessary, and always right, to lean on them.

Open your hand to those who are willing to sincerely give it to you. Hold firm to their grip, and start to take the necessary "baby" steps toward your emotional well-being. Cry when you need to cry, mourn when you need to mourn and feel what you need to feel. But always recognize the progress you make, and understand your ultimate purpose is to learn from your struggle and eventually get back on your *own* two feet.

You must find a healthy way to regain your own stability, because if you choose to cling to the same turmoil (with your feet still and your head hung) your legs will grow weak, you mind will grow stale and your soul will slowly go to sleep. You are the only one who can ultimately walk out of that restricting dark space, and if you allow yourself to stay numb for too long, you will eventually be stuck in the same spot without the strength to move. Choose to progress, not regress, and make your life as good, not as painful, as it can be; life's bumps will supply the pain on their own.

If you choose to wallow in prolonged misery, you literally inhibit happiness from becoming a natural part of your life. You consciously prevent yourself from having positive experiences that will replace what is negative. And if you grasp onto negativity and pain, it is no wonder that negativity and pain will be what you continue to feel. It's like holding onto a hot coal and expecting that your hands will not burn, of course they will burn! The coal is hot, and the longer you hold onto it the deeper the excruciating heat will penetrate! You must begin to acknowledge *your* hot coals, dump them out of your hands and start on your road to healing.

You are the only person in control of your emotions. Other people may do things that affect the way you feel but you, <u>only you</u>, ultimately choose the degree of each feeling you want to hold onto.

Let your soul be inspired! You already have the strength inside you, find it and take that first step. Replace the heavy thoughts, the agony and the continued self-pity with moments, words and actions that are positive. And remember, the minute you start thinking your life is too hard, someone is out there suffering just as much or even more. Find those people and help them. Extend *your* hand. Lend a shoulder and fill up the time you spend reveling in your sorrow, with moments of charity instead. You can do this! You deserve to have a life that is full! One that gives you moments of peace, and gratitude, that you can share with others to help raise them up, not drag them down.

Your thinking dictates your reality...

When you think you must solely carry the burdens that are placed before you and that you are all alone in your life of angst, it becomes easy to shut everyone else out. You don't want to appear weak or fragile so instead of voicing your sadness, you preoccupy yourself with pain and torment and spend your days in silent desperation. When you *think* you are alone, you begin to *feel* like you are alone, and when you *feel* like you are alone, you gradually start to emotionally distance yourself from others. Calls aren't returned, appointments are broken and suddenly you enter into a life of emotional isolation. When in actuality, the purpose of existing, the beautiful reality of living on this planet is that you are *not* alone!

You have the undeniable gift of creating connectedness, and developing personal relationships, that can reinforce the happiness you desire. Start by choosing to believe in something greater than yourself and take solace in something magnificent: God, a higher power, hope, faith, family or a network of women trying to help each other! Find comfort in knowing you are part of something bigger, because you are! Draw from that strength because with a little extra support, you will be able overcome the unbearable sadness that leaves you lonely and face issues that, on your own, seem impossible to confront.

Knowing, and accepting, you are a part of this greater good will also help lead you to an astonishing point of clarity; a moment where you will notice the pain you have been feeling has eased just a little and a smile appears on your face instead of another tear; where your resilience defeats your weakness and your eyes are focused on what is in front of you, not what's been left behind. And when that incredible moment occurs you <u>*will*</u> feel a release. It may be small or it may be life changing but you ***will*** feel it. Pay attention to, and be present in, that moment.

Allow the sensation of release to be the spark that ignites your newfound perspective on life and remember, while you are on your way to that purifying moment of letting go, if you experience anger, frustration or disappointment it is completely natural.

When you awaken buried thoughts, and memories, that have been weighing down your soul, the stirring of these repressed emotions may be accompanied by a residual unpleasantness related to the experiences that created these thoughts, and memories, in the first place. Don't be afraid of what you are feeling; instead, be grateful because now you can acknowledge each of these debilitating emotions and finally put them to rest.

The process is like waking a deadly "monster" who is blocking your passage to a life of peace. The thought in and of itself is frightening, but in order to make it through the passage you have to remove the very obstacle that is blocking your way. Self-doubt, anger, resentment, grief, fear or uncertainty *whatever* is keeping you from experiencing happiness must be confronted; in doing so, it is expected that there will be dust flying, tears shed and a fierce battle with a content monster wanting to stay where it has been comfortably residing for years.

Have a healthy outlet where you can release your negative feelings because they are yours to work through. Your anger is not your husband's, your frustration is not your partner's, your disappointment is not your child's, nor are they your friend's, your co-worker's or your family's. Your low moments are *yours* to own and conquer. Find strength in others, but do not make your turmoil a load they are required to bear. Start writing a journal, paint your emotions on a blank canvas, run, pray, take up kickboxing, tai chi, meditate, find *some kind* of healthy means of releasing any negativity you might be feeling. It will do you, and those around you, a world of good.

Ask for strength, and find a safe place to turn to when you think you can't hold on anymore. Feel secure in the fact that tomorrow is a new day, lean on your hope to make it through times of crisis and embrace the strength that is placed before you. Allow yourself to be open enough to realize what that strength is and when it is given, because when you finally let go of your heartache, your vision will be clearer and your spirit will be brighter. You are meant to be connected to people not isolated, so give yourself the chance! Start by clearing your mind and easing your heart of any unnecessary burden, so that it might lighten and more easily become open to others.

You must give yourself the opportunity to honestly address the quiet battles that afflict you and begin to feel safe in your vulnerability. Once you healthily share your frustration, you will find there are a lot of women out there working through the same dilemmas, but you have to be willing to clean the cobwebs of self-pity from your eyes and openly talk to other women about what gnaws at your soul and prevents you from living a happy life; keeping in mind that the end result is to heal: your mind, your body and your spirit. Through the process, you will be *helping each other.*

Start a support group! Start a carpool! Start sharing your time and resources, and support the women who are working through the same challenges you are. Get involved and contribute some strength to other women, because holding on to your gloom and doom does nothing to make you better. Ask for a little help when you need it, and be there to offer what help you can give.

We all get into funks. Unpredictability happens and always will, but knowing you can rely on a stable group of supportive people can put the unpredictability into perspective: it doesn't have to destroy you. Enjoy your good days and just make it through the bad ones. When life seems to go awry you can either shut down or press forward; it is simply your choice and your happiness will *always* be a direct result of your choices.

Whether you like the concept or not, you will be faced with making some very simple, and terribly complicated, decisions throughout your lifetime. In doing so, you must take the time to honestly evaluate the manner in which you approach a decision that has to be made. Do you have a "knee jerk" response, where the first thought that comes to mind is the response you give? Or are you mindful about weighing the pro's and con's allowing yourself time to assess the situation at hand?

When you are confronted with making a major decision look at it as a wonderful opportunity, and if you begin to feel overwhelmed or unsure, take a deep breath and reach for a piece of paper. Literally write down a list stating the possible positive, and negative, results that could occur from the decision you are about to make. Even though you "think" you have a pretty good mental grasp on what consequences could arise, sometimes actually seeing those results (the good and bad) staring you in the face, creates a clearer view of reality.

If the con column seriously outweighs the pro, you must have enough self-respect, self-control and determination to stick with the decision that will leave you in a better position. Because sometimes, as human beings, we have an amazing capacity to justify anything that will fulfill our own selfish needs, even if it means closing our eyes to what's right in front of us. Commit to making wise, mindful decisions

Seek input from those you trust and be willing to listen to other's opinions. You don't have to necessarily take their advice, you don't have to agree with it and you certainly have no reason to take anything that is said personally, but the perspectives of those close to you might shed some light on different angles, and outcomes, of the decision you are trying to make.

Then finally, after taking time to weigh the pro's and con's, seeking advice from those you trust and honestly listening to your own heart, you will need to make an educated decision and be willing to accept the consequences that follow: good or bad. Because once you decide to make *any* choice, you must commit to it, do it wholeheartedly and not look back. Second guessing yourself is only wasted energy, and once your decision has been made one of two things will happen:

1) It will work out
2) It won't work out

If it works out, GREAT! Enjoy the satisfaction of your effort proving itself to be worthwhile; you made a well thought out decision and the results of your mindful approach ended favorably. If your decision *doesn't* work out, there is no reason to beat yourself up! You made a well thought out decision and the results of your mindful approach did not end favorably; you now have only one constructive option: learn from it and move on.

You cannot go back in time and make different choices. Life doesn't work this way (and thank goodness it doesn't!) because if you *could* go back in time, and try to change the instances or decisions that you thought haven't worked in your favor, instead of discovering your own strength and tenacity in times of struggle or defeat, you would be in a perpetual state of rewind: going back in time to do something better, say something different, do what you "think" would make your present situation better and eventually find yourself in the exact same place, rewinding again.

Accept the consequences that follow after any decision you make because ultimately, every choice you make comes down to one person: you.

You have the final say. If you feel pressured into something, you are the *only* one who either gives into the pressure or you don't. If you have doubt, you are the *only* one who can ask enough questions to gain clarity. If you are confused, you are the *only* one who can get clear or remain in the fog. You cannot blame, or resent, anyone else for the decisions *you* make. They are yours, so take heed in making your decisions wisely.

For example, if you are employed, you had to at some point, **interview** for the job and in order to be in the position you now hold, you had to **first accept** the position when it was offered to you. If you are married, you chose to **say "yes"** to the proposal and **"yes"** at the alter. If you have children, you **engaged in some kind of act** that created a baby. Whether is was sex, adoption or artificial insemination you said **"yes"** the opportunity of inviting a child to be a forever part of your life, and within each of these choices, you can either be grateful or despondent. It is that simple.

So, if you are miserable in any area of your life DO SOMETHING TO MAKE IT BETTER! You really have that power! It is simply a matter of:

1) acknowledging what makes you unhappy
2) deciding how you are going to conquer it
3) finding and using healthy resources that will aid in your healing
4) changing your behavior to create a different way of life.

If you hate your job, start looking for another one! Be responsible for the manner in which you approach the thought of a new career. Again, take the time to make a mindful, responsible decision and plan accordingly. This doesn't mean you should storm out of your office and quit your job immediately (this would fall under the "knee-jerk" category) instead, weigh the pro's and con's and make sure to prepare yourself with some kind of financial back-up. (You could possibly find yourself faced with a period of unemployment.) If you go to, and leave from, your work place in utter despair, it is time to start taking a good look at why you have chosen to spend so much of your lifetime there in the first place.

If you think it is *impossible* to leave your job, then it is time to refocus your perspective, you have to, for the sake of your well-being. You have to force yourself to start finding the good in what makes up your life, and yes, there is *always good to be found*. Choose to make the most of your workplace; you are going to be there anyway. So, make it a place you want to go to and create an environment of motivation. Be grateful you have an income and that you are physically able to work. There are a lot of people in this world who don't have the opportunity.

If you are miserable in your marriage figure out why. You are the one who said yes to this commitment, and the words "I Do" came out of *your* mouth. Choose to start working on a *friendship* with your partner. You committed to spending the rest of your life with this person, now would be a good time to start figuring out why you said yes in the first place. Remind yourself of the qualities in your spouse that you were so drawn to and focus on them. Was it their sense of humor? Compassion? Patience? Intelligence? Revisit the moments in your marriage that have made you smile and focus on *what has been good* in your years together. Then take a deep full breath, a long step back and a good honest look at what *you* are contributing to your marriage. Are you being the kind of spouse you would like to have?

    Relationships are ever changing and you must be able to adapt and grow with the changes that take place, which will hopefully strengthen your marriage. Do things that bring your spouse joy, and each day find at least one way to make them happy; why wouldn't you? This is the person you will be sharing every day of the rest of your life with, so why not help make it pleasant for them and for yourself? Marriage is the strongest partnership you can ever be a part of, but it requires two active participants. You said "yes" to marriage are you saying "yes" to making it work?

    Relationships throughout life, with your friends or family, continually reshape your working model of relationships, it's an ongoing, lifelong process. It is <u>absolutely</u> possible to redirect a relationship that may have veered off course, but the only way to begin the process is to first be willing. This may mean admitting to some of your own mistakes and saying, "I'm sorry."

    However, if you are being physically or mentally abused, GET OUT NOW! There is **nothing** that justifies abuse, and you <u>do not</u> have to be subjected to it. We will explore this more in Chapter 5.

Use your history, as a tool, to learn from your past mistakes, in order to make good present decisions. If, in doing so, you realize you must start over from scratch, it's OK! That is one of the beautiful realities of your life, you can *always* change; you can always do something different.

Base your actions on moments you have been proud of, and work on *not* repeating the moments you haven't been so proud of. Give yourself the opportunity to make choices that leave you joyful.

Hold onto the good memories of the past. There is nothing that can bring friends and loved ones together like creating, and reminiscing about, great times and happy moments. Relive the pleasant moments and then do yourself a big favor, let the ugly ones go! Stop wasting your precious days here reminiscing about a time that no longer exists and focus on what you do have: the present.

You have this moment! You have people in your life! You have today! So make it a day you will pleasantly reflect on when you go to sleep tonight and fill it with moments that will make a positive difference in your life, not a negative one. Use each interaction you have, whether it is with your spouse, a child, a sibling, a friend, a client or the clerk at the grocery store as a moment to create something *good*.

Take a day to be aware of what happens around you. Are the conversations you engage in sincere? Do the thoughts that plague your mind pertain to ideas that, in the grand scheme of things, really matter? When was the last time you took five minutes to really BREATHE? Your life is what you make it, it really is. Are you making it the kind of life that allows you the opportunity to be open to others and safe in your own being? Or, are you so consumed with heartache and guilt from the past, that you have literally shut yourself off from the present?

The Martyr

The past does not exist. Conditions that have arisen from past choices you have made may exist, but the actual past does not. You cannot go back to it, and you cannot do it over; it is what it is: OVER. The only place the past lives is in your mind.

Stop beating yourself up over the would've, should've and could've because the time, the moment and the situation no longer exist. There is absolutely no way to determine how your life could have turned out if you would have done something different, said something different or chosen a different path. You are exactly where you are suppose to be right now, because it is exactly where you are. You can't be anywhere else or you would be. You shouldn't be with anyone else or you would be. Most importantly, you can't be anyone else or you would be, and you're not, **you're you**: your beautiful, authentic, own unique self!

Choose to *not be* preoccupied with past hurt and sorrow, in lieu of the new day that is happening right in front of you. A day that, if you allow, can be made into a stepping stone toward a better place. Really think about where the path of choices you are laying is leading you, because each thought you have and every action you make is creating your life.

"...one cannot lodge in if."
~Rumi

Chapter 4

The Appeaser

4

"Our lives begin to end the day we become silent about the things that matter."

~Martin Luther King, Jr.

*W*e know who we are...

...the women who will go along with everyone else, even if we have a different opinion, desire or idea. Our go to phrase is "Oh, I don't care, whatever you want." Our viewpoints sway depending on our company. We certainly wouldn't want to ruffle anyone's feathers, and we certainly wouldn't want to end up not liked by anyone. We don't disagree because we would hate to be the result of any kind of tension, and we will bite our tongue, until it bleeds, before entertaining the thought of saying something that might spark a debate. To us, debate is confrontation, confrontation is dissension and dissent is something we never want to be a part of.

We think it is more important to make sure everyone else feels OK rather than speak about something that would make *us* feel better, and even if it means not speaking the truth, we tell people what they want to hear. We rarely, *if ever*, ask for help because we wince at the thought of "inconveniencing" anyone.

We are a mysterious paradox to those close to us: we are always helping others while slowly killing ourselves on the inside, we are socially agreeable yet emotionally chaotic. No one knows how we sincerely feel about anything. We have lost the freedom in speaking our true beliefs because we have allowed them to be shaped by everyone else's. It is only through the acceptance, and approval, of others that we feel validated.

Our dreams are silent, our ideas are never expressed and our contained frustration continues to pile onto our soul. We have forgotten how important our true voice is, because we don't even know what it sounds like anymore.

Your voice is the gateway to your intriguing mind and beautiful soul. The time has come to unlock the gate and let the abundance of your important words flow.

As an appeaser, you may often monitor what you say based on an illusion: if *your* thoughts -and words- don't agree with the consensus of opinion you might upset someone or make them angry. So, you choose to remain quiet as not to, inadvertently, hurt anyone's feelings; it's a safer option. But guess what? If your opinion causes someone else to feel uncomfortable, THAT'S THEIR PROBLEM! Not yours.

Any statement you make, will always have a side that agrees and a side that disagrees. The point of using your voice is not to please everyone else; the point is to sincerely express what you think and what you feel. If you walk through this world reluctant to share your honest thoughts and opinions, you might as well stop talking all together. Because when you refuse to speak your mind, in an effort to please or save someone, you end up neglecting someone else: yourself. You were put here to make a positive difference. How can you possibly do that if everything you want to say is monitored by fear?

Fear is one of the most intense emotions you will experience, from it you be forced to find your courage and strength, you will learn to either fight or flee and sometimes, because of fear, you will be forced to address situations and circumstances you would otherwise avoid. But just because you fear something does not mean you have to be controlled by it.

Fear is powerful and can be the most restricting emotion you can allow yourself to succumb to, but thankfully, it can always be stymied by first; addressing, head-on, exactly that which you fear and second, finding a healthy way to overcome it. If you are afraid of expressing your thoughts, the only way to conquer that fear is to start talking!

One of the greatest gifts you can ever give yourself, is to learn how to effectively communicate. There is absolutely nothing wrong with expressing your true feelings, ideas, concerns and wants. What is important, however, is to be clear in the the way you express them, because it's not always about *what* you have to say but -more importantly- *how clearly* you say it.

If you are happy, SAY SO! If you are unhappy, SAY SO! Again, you are a beautifully emotional creature who *feels* an ocean of emotions, so it is expected you would want to express the ebb and flow. Give yourself necessary time and space to figure out what you are really feeling, because when you allow yourself, even a moment, to collect and organize your thoughts you can more conscientiously -and accurately- communicate what it is you are truly feeling. Which will leave less room for confusion, doubt or misunderstanding.

Gain clarity, in what stirs your soul, and if you can't put a finger on what you are feeling say, "I am not exactly sure what I am feeling, I need some time to sift through it and figure it out." Instead of letting thoughts spew from your mouth, take the time to be aware of what you are thinking, decide what you want to say and then be straightforward. Give yourself a moment to take a deep breath before you make a statement or express a concern. It does wonders!

Be concise with your words. You cannot expect anyone to interpret what you are saying or to "just know" what you are feeling. No one is a mind reader, and as much as we would like for mental telepathy to be a natural part of our relationships, it's not. You cannot assume anyone *knows* what is going on, inside your mind or spirit, without expressing it; just as you cannot assume *you* know what anyone else is thinking or feeling, without *them* expressing it to you.

We've all been in a situation where what we've said, we thought the other person understood when what they said, about what they heard us say, had nothing to do with what we thought or said (see what I mean). Interpretations of other's actions and statements can lead to confusion and terrible inaccuracy, so be inquisitive. If you are not sure about something...ask. If you feel like you are being misunderstood... clarify. Make eye contact with the people you talk to, speak your mind and be honest and precise about what you are feeling. Simplify your relationships by engaging in healthy, comprehensible communication. Ask, speak and listen with sincerity.

Bring awareness to the way you vocalize your thoughts. What tone do you use? Do you whisper or do you shout? For one day, really pay attention to the way you engage in conversation. Are you nervous or relaxed? Are you engrossed or is your mind wandering? Are you expressing what you truly feel or do your words cater to the needs of the person you are conversing with?

There are numerous resources available to you about learning how to speak with confidence, from on-line courses to books, classes and workshops. The support is ready and waiting for you. Learn something new about the way you communicate and then practice, because there is always a choice in the way you express yourself and you are the *only one* in control of what you ask for and simply say.

You can communicate a concern curtly as easily as you can gently. You do not have to be demanding in asking for something, or for clarification, but you can be firm. You can purposefully ask for what you want without nagging by just simply *asking* , but results will not materialize if you bottle up your desires and keep your words mum. If you choose to *not* put a voice to your thoughts they will only end up being just that: **thoughts**, cluttering your mind without purpose or direction.

Start to recognize the way you verbally relate to others. Are your experiences usually positive or do they, more often, have a negative undertone? When you can construct your conversations from thoughts, words and expressions that are positive and concise, you will be more likely to engage in good, productive communication. Remember, *what you give is what you get.*

Start small. Initiate conversation with your neighbors, or talk to people you wouldn't normally strike up a conversation with at work. While at the grocery store, actually look the attendant in the eye, smile and say thank you. If you are in a relationship, share with your partner that you are going to work on refining your communication skills. Let them know it will take some time and dedication but that you are embarking on a new journey of positive, constructive communication. Sincerely ask for their patience and support because in the long run, it will do you both a great amount of good.

Start making simple connections that spark healthy, sincere conversation. Of course it may feel uncomfortable at first, you are doing something new, but after a little practice you will feel more secure in the way you verbally communicate. You will begin to recognize what your true voice sounds like and revel in the joy of your new found confidence. You are meant to connect, and the more you articulate your thoughts, engage in healthy conversation and confidently express your ideas and feelings, you will become more at ease in doing so. Speak honestly and *really* listen; before you know it, conversing will be enjoyable and much more meaningful.

There are two components that make up successful communication: speaking *and* listening. It is impossible to be an effective communicator if you only do one and not the other. Take a day to observe the way you listen to other people. Do you interrupt? Are you *really* willing to hear what someone has to say? Do you welcome a contradictory opinion? Your observations may surprise you.

A common dilemma (we have all experienced when listening to someone) is getting lost in your own thoughts while someone else is speaking. If your attention is only on what is happening in your own mind, it will be impossible to be fully engaged in a conversation where you are suppose to be an active participant.

Slow down your thought process and focus on whomever is speaking to you. Calm your mind and concentrate only on what is being said. Simplify your life, and conversations, by being present in each moment and by *really* hearing what words are being spoken. You are in control of your thoughts, and if you find them wandering, reel them back in to the conversation at hand!

When you become overwhelmed with other's opinions (whether you agree with them or not) it can be easy to instantly "tune them out" the moment they open their mouth to speak. Maybe this reaction kicks in because they don't know when to stop talking, or maybe the conversations are always one sided, but regardless of the justification you must reach a point where you feel comfortable in making statements like, "I feel like there is nothing more that needs to be said," "I will not engage in hurtful conversation," or "I do not appreciate the negative things you say to me." Understand that you are capable of taking control of a situation that makes you uncomfortable, but, in order to do so, you must be constructive with your words and express what you are honestly feeling.

If you have developed a defense mechanism that simply tunes others out, and disconnects you from a conversation that is taking place, you are not attending to the care of your soul. There is a reason you are "tuning out" and, for the sake of your well-being, you must confront your unease. Why you don't want to hear what this person has to say? Are their words spiteful or malicious? Are you simply not interested? Are you intimidated? Get to the root of your emotion. If speaking to a particular person actually causes you emotional distress, you have two choices:

1) address your uncomfortableness
2) disassociate yourself from that person.

If you choose to address the unease, first: honestly reflect on why you feel this way. Is this person demeaning or condescending? Are they self-absorbed? Are you able to get a word in edgewise? Prepare yourself by formulating a thought-out, concise explanation as to why you feel uncomfortable, clearly address the issue and express your concern. Once you speak your mind about resolving the communication barrier that causes you distress, one of three things will happen:

1) the situation will improve
2) the situation will not improve
3) the situation will be worse than it was before

Regardless of the outcome, you, at the very least, will have expressed your concern, done what you could to make it better and will have courageously responded to an issue that has caused you unease. After you have vocalized your desire to fix the situation, you will have one decision to make: continue to resolve the tension or simply say good-bye.

If you continue to hold your thoughts and emotions inside, without offering them a source of release, you will become emotionally clogged. You will become so overloaded with thought and emotion, that you will not know how to accurately identify the emotion you are truly feeling; which leads to anxiety, frustration and terrible internal discord Eventually, you will shut down.

Your voice can only be deprived for so long. Your heart can only be so heavy, before it begins to sink, and without expressing your honest hopes, dreams, fears and ideas your mind will become filled with dust from the stale thoughts that remain trapped inside. Be safe in asking. Be safe in saying and be safe in finding clarity. Your mind must be clear in order to differentiate between: accurate thoughts about yourself, your relationships and everything going on around you and unsubstantiated thoughts that are fueled by chaotic emotion. The choice is yours to either keep your mind clear or to leave it in a hazy fog.

When you feel strongly about what you believe, it can be easy to become frustrated if you are conversing with someone who doesn't agree with what you have to say. Usually when this happens, it is because your emotions override the meaning of what you are trying to convey. These moments provide a perfect opportunity to take a looonnng breath, slow down your thought process and simply listen.

Everyone is entitled to an opinion and when they have one, if it does not coincide with yours, don't take it personally! Their opinion is theirs to own. It doesn't mean their thoughts or words are any more valuable than yours -and it doesn't mean they are necessarily right or wrong- but their words are their thoughts. And in having honest dialog, you must be able to give your opinion as well as listen to someone else's. That is communication: the **successful** conveying of **sharing** ideas or feelings. Not only when you speak, but also when you listen.

Respond to others the same way you would like others to respond to you: with intention and respect. This does not mean you have to agree with every word or opinion that is offered, but in order to be heard you must reciprocate with mindful listening. You can still have meaningful relationships with people who have differing opinions. Believe in what you say, own your ideas and if the rest of the world doesn't agree with you, it's OK. You don't agree with everyone else either.

Be confident in your position and knowledgeable enough to defend your convictions, of course you would never want to *intentionally* hurt someone (refer to chapter 7), but other people will process the information you give them through their own method of reasoning.

We each have our unique view of this world and the people we observe in it. We all have minds, but they each think differently; we all have ideas, but they stem from different inspiration. Our varying viewpoints are what keep this world fascinating and everyone is entitled to express their own interpretation of it, including you. We do not have to always agree, but we should all have an opportunity to be heard. Open up about how you feel, be honest with other people and, most importantly, be honest with yourself!

"Knee jerk reactions", within any context, are emotionally charged reactions and do not usually produce healthy results. So, if someone upsets you, before making any assumptions, take the time to first get to the root of <u>why</u> you are upset. Did they say, or do, something that made you uncomfortable, angry or sad? Address your concerns honestly, speak to the source and be specific about what is troubling you.

Don't let doubt devour your spirit put a voice to it instead! If you are unclear about the motivation for someone's actions, ask them about it. If you are concerned about a conversation that has taken place, address it. Harboring doubt is unfair to you and unfair to the person you are doubting. Dig to the root of what is really disturbing you, develop a constructive way to address your concern and then simply ask if there is any merit to what you are feeling. Resolve the doubt and move on. It is that simple.

There are probably a handful of people you have counted on in your life to offer frank and honest opinions. Even in situations where you haven't wanted to hear the truth, they have loved you enough, and cared enough about your well-being, to help pick you up when you were down; say "no" when you wanted "yes," "yes" when you wanted "no," and understood when words weren't needed at all. They are still around after the turbulence, the happiness, the time together and the time apart. Their opinion matters and you trust them. They share in your misfortune as well as your success, and you love them for it. You may have one person like this in your life -or there might be many- but it isn't the number that matters, it is the quality. Through the years, these beautiful souls always remain.

Let this inner circle of trust, and love, remind you of what is important and what is real; we waste too much time trying to satisfy other's expectations of us. Stop falling into the trap, instead just be you and surround yourself with people you respect, people you admire and people you trust. Allow those who are close to you, the opportunity to keep you grounded and in check. That's what people who care about you are suppose to do. They are there to help bring you back down to earth if you ever set yourself afloat; they love you enough to be honest with you. So, be grateful for them and take care of them, just as they take care of you! Cultivate and maintain these honest relationships because this is where pure love thrives.

There are a lot of good people in this world! Use your voice to thank those who have made a positive impact on your life. Pick up the phone and give them a call, write a heartfelt letter or make a personal visit. They deserve to know that their time here has mattered and that their influence, whether they are aware of it or not, has made an undeniable difference. It's easy to take for granted that those who have inspired, encouraged, cared for and motivated you already know how grateful you are, but even if they do, take the time to graciously remind them of your thanks.

Acknowledge those who continue to enhance the lives of others by being exactly who they are and by simply doing the small things (you know a few of these people). Put a voice to your admiration for others and never miss an opportunity to express your gratitude and appreciation. Make your life a reflection of the good that has affected you. Devote your energy and your words to creating a good life for _you_ and as a result, you will be creating goodness and light in the lives of those who surround you.

In striving to maintain a life of speaking honestly and living positively, please keep in mind that although you can be an example of what is good, healthy and real, you are not responsible for rescuing others from their own demise; not only are you not responsible for their rescue, you couldn't do it anyway.

Be gentle to others and be kind. Offer words and acts of encouragement and have compassion for those who might be suffering. Relate to those that may be going through a similar experience you have survived, whether it is a tragedy or triumph, because that's what we are here to do: to connect with each other and to give to each other. You can offer peace, offer a hand, offer your friendship and sympathy but each one of us must ultimately choose, for ourselves, what kind of life we really want to live.

You cannot *force* anyone to change their life. It is not your place nor is it your responsibility. But the beauty that comes from choosing to live a life of balance, and wellness, is that the goodness you create is simply contagious. Happiness begets happiness.

The feeling of unconditional love fuels the soul and silently encourages us to be easier on each other, and challenges us to be better human beings. This is why optimism and compassion are so powerful; they also stimulate the goodness in our souls.. Do not judge anyone based on the way they look, by the way they dress, by the way they speak or by their circumstances. You never know where someone has started and you never know where they may end up. Use your power to create an environment of good, and motivation, for those who surround you and, as a result, you will help others *feel* good and *feel* motivated.

We all have the will to choose, but you are responsible for <u>you</u>. And from that responsibility, you either influence others through what is positive and healthy or through what is negative and unhealthy. You cannot *force* anyone to change, and you cannot rescue anyone from self-destruction. They must ultimately decide to do it for themselves. What you *can do* is provide support and encouragement because, sometimes, just knowing that someone sincerely believes in you, is all it takes to spark the desire to change your life.

Open your mind and start speaking about what inspires you because your mind is meant to be used, to grow and expand. Develop a creative outlet of expression. Instead of keeping your thoughts locked inside, release them through writing, drawing, dancing, encouraging, organizing, developing, speaking, helping, *anything* healthy, because if you are holding back any part of who you are: your wants, your gratitude, your abilities or your unhappiness, you are only limiting the growth of your mind and spirit. You are denying our world of your incredible influence.

A fantastic method of negative emotional release is to take a piece of paper and write a letter. The intent isn't to actually send the letter, it is to help unleash the festering emotional issues you haven't been able to resolve. Write as though you are actually talking to the person, place or event that has caused you prolonged hurt and heartache. Use no refrain in describing every bit of anger, sadness, confusion and blame that you have felt, and when you are finished writing, whether the letter is one page or one-hundred pages, tear it into tiny pieces and then do the following:

1) burn the pieces of paper and watch your words, heartache and anger go up in flames

(and of course do this in a responsible, controlled manner, adhering to all safety precautions)

In watching the pages slowly disintegrate and finally disappear, visualize the crippling emotion you have been harboring disintegrate and disappear as well. It will be magnificent and you will feel incredible!

Use your imagination and open yourself up to great possibilities! Begin to explore new avenues to replace any negativity you are experiencing with thoughts, and activities, that are positive. Take a half hour out of your TV watching schedule and read about an unfamiliar topic you wouldn't normally spend time on. Start exercising your mind because it's been proven that the more you put it to work, the better it will run and from a scientific standpoint, new brain cells either become integrated or die off. If you work on forming new memories, you directly enhance the likelihood that new neurons will remain in the brain. USE YOUR MARVELOUS MIND!

Educate yourself about current events, and develop a *personal* understanding of the world around you to share with others. Learn something about another country, art, music, your ancestors, politics or sports! Open yourself up to an unfamiliar topic that you wouldn't normally spend your time on. Be passionate about *something* and start talking about what moves you, because sharing your opinion sparks conversation, conversation sparks ideas and ideas spark change. Vocalize what you visualize and your life **will** begin to take a new form. Your opinions matter, your ideas matter and your voice matters! Speak up!

"It's not the critic who counts, not the man who points out how the strong man stumbled, or when the doer of deeds could have done better.
The credit belongs to the man who is actually in the arena; whose face is marred by dust and sweat and blood; who strives valiantly; who errs and comes short again and again; who knows the great enthusiasms, the great devotions and spends himself in a worthy cause; who at the best, knows in the end the triumph of high achievement; and who at the worst if he fails, at least fails while daring greatly,
so that his place shall never be with those cold and timid souls who live in the gray twilight that knows neither victory nor defeat."

~Theodore Roosevelt

Chapter 5

The I Just Can't Win

5

*"If one advances confidently in the direction of one's dreams,
and endeavors to live the life which one has imagined,
one will meet with a success unexpected in common hours."*
~Henry David Thoreau

*W*e know who we are...

the women who can't get on top. We take two steps forward and, inevitably, a crisis occurs and we're five steps back. We just can't get ahead. We are constantly slammed with all the tough breaks, no one understands us and we are tired of always getting the raw end of the deal. Most of our life has been a struggle, whether it's been personal, financial or physical and the cause of our turmoil has always been someone else's fault. Our parents didn't raise us properly. Our siblings always had better. Our "friends" aren't people we can sincerely trust and our bosses have all been jerks. It's not our fault that everyone is out to get us. Life just isn't fair.

Nothing works out the way we plan and nothing works out in our favor. We battle through this hell alone, and no one will give us that one chance we need to break through. We're sick of seeing others succeed when all we do is fail. Why bother trying anymore? If only others could live our life for one day they would see how hard it really is. We have resigned ourselves to the undeniable fact that life is miserable and always will be. Nothing *ever* goes right. We continue to fall into the same cycles and our life continues to unfold the same way...the way that hasn't been working.

*But you have so much to offer this world! The time has come to take control of your life and you are the **only** one who can do just that.*

What you choose to focus on is what you will get. If you want love, you have to be love. If you want success, you have to be success and if you want honesty, you have to be honest. When you choose to make your actions, interactions and behavior a reflection of who it is you want to become, amazingly you are that person.

Your brain is a fascinating, incredibly complex and oh, so powerful control center. If you choose to, you have the capability to *actually change* the way you physically, and emotionally, respond to the world around you; and like most worthwhile things in this lifetime, it takes honest, consistent, determined work. Completely changing your perspective and behavior isn't easy, but it is certainly possible and worth more to the quality of your life than you could ever imagine.

When your mind thinks one thing it is very difficult for your body to express something else; completely changing your perception of life can be compared to learning to speak a new language: it must be *practiced* and *reinforced* using the proper language. For example, if you are learning to speak Italian and practice words that are Russian, Hindi and Japanese you will be utterly confused and further from mastering the language of Italian than when you started. Not only will you end up confused, but you'll also be frustrated and likely, resort to the comfortable, familiar language you already spoke with ease. The same kind of interaction takes place with your mind and your actions.

The language your mind speaks is the language your body and spirit respond to. If you are constantly telling yourself how unhappy you are, you are going to be unhappy. If you are constantly blaming the world for all of your problems, the world will continue to give you problems. If you constantly think about how tired you are, you are going to be tired. You are not allowing yourself to be programmed for anything else!

The definition of insanity (according to Albert Einstein) is "doing the same thing over and over and expecting different results," and if you are caught in a destructive cycle of thought and action, do you really wonder why the same terrible things keep happening to you? It is not a mystery. Start living a new language! One that sees the good surrounding you, the opportunities in any challenge and speaks optimism and growth! What you choose to focus on is what you will get. Break the destructive cycle and create something original!

Embracing a new way of life might be a difficult change for you because the negativity may be all you know, but even though the transformation may seem difficult, it is not impossible! *You deserve to have a life full of happiness and a foundation of positive self-worth.* It is your inherent purpose to enjoy this lifetime and all the beauty it has to offer. The very core of your being is made up of that pure love and beauty! But if you are surrounded by nothing but cynicism, and if the dissent is a constant fixture in you life, it is no wonder that the negativity is more familiar to you and that you continue to reside in what is negative.

The self-doubt and cop-outs may have been handed down from generations of women, to generations of other women in your family. The negativity may be what you have seen and heard growing up and continues to surround you in your adult life. Are these women in your life to blame for your unhappiness? Absolutely not! They are each on their own path and have lived, and are choosing to live, the lives that they have come to know as familiar. But you have the wonderful opportunity to learn from them and change in <u>you</u> what is keeping your life frozen. And a good first step would be to:

recognize the relationships you have developed throughout your lifetime and take inventory of the kind of people you attract and are drawn to.

Acknowledge if these relationships are rooted in negativity or positivity and observe what you are surrounded by, because the amazing power you have, in making personal choices, means you do not have to pass on the historic cynicism. You can reverse the pessimistic view of this world that has been a natural part of your existence and it is entirely your choice. **You can break the cycle**. You just need to decide this is what you want to do and take control of the choices you make.

Your life is *yours* to sculpt and point in a direction of happiness, achievement and enjoyment, rooted from the very essence of simply being you. So, make today the first day of your transformation!

Second step in creating a new life:

honestly accept giving up what is not working.

Start with the simple things:

1) Your sleeping habits: they can affect your happiness, physical health and mental well-being dramatically. Give yourself a bed time (just

like your children) and make it realistic. A time you can aim for, at a decent hour, that will allow at least six to eight hours of sleep every night (not four or ten). You must reprioritize your life and allow consistent time for rest; you have to! This may mean cutting out an hour of television or scheduling one less meeting to attend. Set a goal for five nights a week. You *have* to start reprogramming you mind and your body.

2) Your home: get rid of your clutter! It is time to change what has not been working. Start throwing out furniture, clothes, books, magazines, pots, pans, artwork, memorabilia, dishes and anything else you are holding onto that serves no purpose. Learn to detach yourself from "things." They are not you and you are not them. View this cleansing symbolically: you are ridding yourself of old, stale and limiting clutter just as you are ridding yourself of an old, stale and limiting way of life. Give your goods to a local charity, not only will you be clearing your place of sanctity, you will be offering something to those in need (refer to Chapter 10). Your home is a place that should be nourishing and calm. Clean it up because your surroundings will always affect the way you feel!

3) Your time: use you minutes, hours and days wisely. Fill up your moments with activities that lead you in a direction you are excited about, not a direction you are always complaining about. Stop engaging in activities that aren't helping you reach your goals. Ask yourself daily, "is what I am doing right now, (whether it is a conversation, physical activity, diet, sleep, help, prayer, travel, etc.) adding goodness to my life and making other's lives better, or is is creating havoc?" If it is a detriment, get rid of it!

When you start filling your life with positive change, everything else settles into place. It really does! But if you continue to blame the world for your misery and everyone else for your unhappiness, you give the world and everyone else complete control over your emotions.

> *"God, grant me the serenity to accept the things I cannot change,*
> *The courage to change the things I can,*
> *And the wisdom to know the difference."*
> ~The Serenity Prayer

One aspect of your life you *cannot* change is the way you were raised. The process is over, finished, complete and you are now an adult.

There are those of you who had a tragic childhood plagued by mistrust, fear and emotional or physical abandonment. None of it is right and none of it is excusable. Children need stability, comfort, love and acceptance in order to thrive, and if you have *ever* suffered any abuse or neglect please understand, your tragedy and turmoil have shaped you but they ***do not define you***.

You deserve to have a life free from the demons you have fought since your childhood. Healing festering, emotional wounds may require some help and you certainly do not have to face the demons alone. Please talk to someone. Whether it is a psychotherapist, a behavioral therapist, a substance abuse consoler or a religious leader find an outlet that is comfortable for you and a place where you feel safe in releasing your pain. Experiences from the past do not have to hinder your future progress but in order to heal a wound, you must first acknowledge that it exists.

The time has come to say good-bye to the oppressiveness of your past and learn how to make your life better. Make a decision to resolve the issues that leave you angry because once you recognize your pain you then have two choices:

1) allow yourself to steer in a direction that gives you the opportunity to heal
2) continue to live in your darkness

It is up to you.

When you begin to take the necessary steps toward your emotional, mental and physical restoration, focus on the positive lessons you learned from your parents. Embrace the moments in your past that give you peace and the aspects of your childhood that have made you the individual you are today. Thank your parents for giving you life, and thank them for the sacrifices they made to ensure your well-being. Whether is was something as simple as keeping you fed to something as enormous as saving your life. Thank them.

We can be quick to criticize our parents and blame them for miserable circumstances that were out of our control as children, but it seems that appreciation for what got us here and gratitude for the simple things they did for us are not discussed as much. Your parents had a childhood as well, and their lives might have been peppered with ugliness and sadness, leaving them with their own deep, unresolved wounds. Take the time to compassionately reflect on the hurdles they had to overcome. They are human too.

You didn't make into this world on your own and whether you had a glorious or terrible childhood, your parents did the best they could or knew how. Right now, in the present, you have the incredible opportunity to learn from them, how or how not to live, and then take full control and responsibility for the substance of your own life. Free yourself from the terrible hindrance of resentment; instead, give credit where credit is due. Forgiveness will be your emotional salvation.

The time has come to start becoming the woman you have always known is inside you. The direction of your path is up to one person: you! If you think your insecurities stem from your rearing, realize the power you have within you to prevent those instances from stifling who you are right now. No one else has control of your being unless you allow them that right. If you need to settle a strained relationship, now is the time to do so. Waiting one more day will only add one more day of unease to your life. So, make it a day of empowerment! Take the energy you expend on focusing on your dysfunctional past and instead use it to mend what has been keeping you broken.

Think of the total number of minutes you have spent dissecting what "could have" and "should have" been done for you. Do the minutes add up to hours? Days? Years? You have spent enough energy on a time that no longer exists. Blaming the past for your present misery does nothing to change your present misery.

Use the precious moments you *do* have to focus on what is good in your life, because there is *always* something good to recognize. And if you don't think so...*make* something good happen and change the way your thoughts always lead back to your rearing.

When you find yourself blaming your parents for the unhappiness you experience in your adult life, **stop**. Literally tell yourself, aloud, to "stop" and that "**I am the one who is in control of my present life**." Redirect your focus and rebuild the dark, fractured space that harbors your hostility into something light and whole.

*You are in control of your choices and
you are in control of your life.*

Then, most importantly, start creating a new healthy cycle. If you become a mother, be the kind of parent who is responsible for ensuring a stable, healthy, loving environment for the children you decide to have. It takes one act to bring a child into this world, so *if you engage in that act* be aware of the responsibilities that could most certainly ensue.

Being a parent will be the most difficult and rewarding job you will ever have. Yes, JOB. It is your duty to give your children a foundation built from responsibility, consistency, example, discipline and love. And it is *crucial* you live *your* life in the manner that reflects what you expect them to learn. This does not mean you must strive to be the "perfect" parent or have "perfect" children (it's not possible anyway, refer to Chapter 8). What *is* important, however, is to teach them to respect their parents, to respect other people and to respect themselves. You already have inside you all that is necessary to be a good mother. Be healthy and happy and your children will thrive. You bring your children into this world, do not make their lives miserable just because you think you are.

Children need consistency and stability. Give them an opportunity to succeed and be aware of the vital importance of good, responsible parenting. We all have our up days, we all have our down days but the bottom line is that you are responsible for your child's life. It is *essential* they are provided with an environment of encouragement, hope, discipline and love. Be involved and be consistent in raising them, because once you bring a tender, vulnerable, pure soul into this world you have two choices:

1) be the best parent you can be
2) don't be the best parent you can be

And if you choose the latter, STOP MAKING BABIES.

One of the constant complaints made by women is "there just aren't any good men out there." When in actuality, that's not the case. But if you really believe that in this world of over two billion men, there isn't **one** good man left, then what kind of man do you honestly think you are going to attract?

Your thinking dictates your reality.

What person, in their right mind, would want to enter into a relationship that is already plagued with suspicion and immediately have to defend themselves for simply being who they are? A good rule of thumb for ANY relationship: If you are going to expect the worst in someone don't be surprised if that's *exactly* what you end up getting.

Would you like to have a partner who is kind, intelligent, motivated, successful and happy? Then BE THAT PERSON! You gravitate to, and attract, likeness and an imbalance in your life will occur if you have expectations of everyone else that you aren't willing to live up to yourself. This includes friends, husbands, wives, partners, mothers, fathers, children, coworkers, priests/pastors... EVERYONE. We are human beings. We are not perfect and we are all unique. The only consideration you should have about a potential partner is: "Are they honest and can I be honest with them?" "Can I trust them and can they trust me?" and most importantly, "Do we bring out what is good in each other?" You have to be willing to give what is good in order to receive what is good. Period.

Start taking responsibility for your actions. For example, when you wake up in the morning what's the first thing you do? Say to yourself how tired you are? Mumble about how badly you hate your job or the person you're waking up to? Or do you take five minutes to stretch, say a prayer or express how grateful you are for having a bed to sleep in, a roof to cover your head and fresh air to breathe?

Through your state of mind and actions, you choose to start your day off miserably or peacefully; your misery comes from your own well of emotion. Your morning, your day and your life is what you make it and if you are miserable, do something to change it!

Recreate the morning rituals that have conditioned your body, mind and soul.

Start with how you wake up. If you use an alarm clock, change the sound of the alarm. Refrain from hitting the snooze button, get a comfortable set of slippers, keep the lights dim until you are out of the shower, tell yourself (even if you are miserable doing it) that you are grateful for the day you are about to begin and force yourself to smile (at least once) while in the shower. Start a new routine! Change your behavior and you *will* change your life. Just try it.

Take a moment to think about someone who inspires you, whether it is a role model, a friend or a leader and specifically address what have they done, in their life, to create the admiration and respect you feel for them. Have they risen above dire circumstances to fulfill their greatest dreams? Because it happens, and it happens to those who have a vision, a desire and belief that they will do what it takes to experience what is good in this lifetime. Their focus is directed on only what they will accept for their life and their future: nothing short of wonderful, nothing short of incredible and nothing short of everything they have imagined their life to be. They take action!

Find someone you admire and learn from them. Be inspired by their perseverance and strength, because it's in you too! Make choices that lead you in a direction of happiness, compassion and achievement. It is up to you. You are capable of becoming your best self where you can appreciate the beautiful life <u>you</u> have created.

If you are unhappy about where you are in life, stop living your life the way you've always lived it and start living the life you really want to have. It is that simple. Redirect your perspective and change your simple actions. Create new habits and new routines by consciously forming new thoughts and behavior, and as a result you will literally create a new life.

"The most effective way to do it, is to do it."
~Amelia Earhart

Chapter 6

The Brooder

6

"...if something can be done to fix a situation,
there is no need to worry,
whereas on the other hand,
if there is nothing that can be done,
there is no use in worrying."

~Shantideva

*W*e know who we are...

    the women who are always on edge, unnerved and ready to break at any moment. When someone sincerely asks how we are, we instantly fight the urge to cry. Our minds won't stop racing. If we have a moment of peace, it comes to an abrupt halt due to the constant worry of what others might be thinking, wondering if we look right, hoping we haven't offended anyone or reminders of everything that makes us sad. We worry if we don't have something to worry about. We are ready to collapse emotionally, mentally and physically, but are afraid that if anyone knows about our inner pandemonium we will just make them worry.

    The bags under our eyes reflect our lack of sleep due to our nights of agonizing about all that needs to be done, all that wasn't done, wondering if everyone else is OK and being unsettled because we aren't sleeping. We are exhausted and our attention span is limited. Everyone around us feels, and knows, that emotionally we are fifty percent available one-hundred percent of the time. We're not really hiding our internal unrest from anyone, but others are baffled about how to break through. We are lost in some other moment, in some other place and in some other emotion, missing the very moment, place and emotion of right now.

The time has come to calm your frenetic mind and still your unsettled soul.

    We have all had an instant where we questioned our own sanity (and for some of us, it's been more than just "an" instant). We wonder if we are in the right place, viewing life clearly and headed in the right direction.

    Self reflection is one of the most important tools for growth, and it is crucial for your betterment to allow yourself the opportunity to honestly contemplate who you are and what you give to this world. That's what growth is: the process of developing mentally, physically and spiritually. Give yourself the space, and time, to reflect and openly search for ways to be better. Honestly reevaluate your goals, your desires and your place in this world. But when doing so keep in mind, there is a BIG difference between self reflection and brooding.

    To brood is to think deeply about something that makes you unhappy, and when you are consumed with worry and constantly think about things that bring you gloom (or the "possibility" of events that might not even taken place) you hinder your ability to become brilliant. When you worry, you suffocate the progress inside you that so desperately wants to surface. You make your life more complicated, instead of more simple, by adding issues to your thought process that do nothing to make you better.

Worry creates unnecessary physical stress on your body, and when you are in a worrisome state of mind, your emotional state becomes frantic and distracts your soul from recognizing and feeling peace. Brooding and worry do not play in any part of constructive progress.

Development happens when change happens, and you have to be willing to alter parts of yourself in order to grow. A crucial element of this process includes letting go of past events, past emotions and present hang-up's. It's like the same technique used in pruning a plant.

Pruning is necessary, in order to increase the fruitfulness and growth of a plant. And if you want your plant to thrive, you must get rid of the dysfunctional parts that do not serve a healthy purpose. Dead or overgrown branches, that take energy away from the healthier core of the plant, must be cut off. The same principle can be applied to *you*.

To achieve mental and spiritual growth, you must rid yourself of dysfunctional behavior that sucks energy from your soul: negative self talk, judgment of others, an unhealthy lifestyle and worry. The moments you spend on worry are moments you could be using to blossom. How much energy do you spend ruminating on what creates your gloom?

When you hold onto thoughts of sadness and repeat them over and over in your mind, your expended energy does not serve a healthy purpose. When you brood, you choose to live a life of worry and a life of worry only creates a life of unease, for you and everyone around you. So, why not choose to make your life one of calm instead?

It is not your natural state to feel stressed, depressed or overwhelmed and if you *are* feeling a devastating degree of any of these emotions, GET HELP! It's OK to talk to someone.

We are meant to connect.

Unfortunately, having therapy for any emotionally related issue still holds some kind of stigma. There needn't be because therapy, if used properly, is a wonderful tool for attaining mental and emotional health. At the very least, it can provide a safe haven to unload the emotional debris you have been stockpiling and teach you how to redirect your thought process from hoarding negative, debilitating thoughts. It takes a person with determination and strength to recognize, and take advantage of, the unlimited capabilities therapy has to offer.

Purging your worry is one of the most effective ways to begin healing; once you address your specific preoccupations, you will then have an opportunity to start organizing them. Some will be thrown in the dumpster immediately, while others will require very close inspection, but if you resist acknowledging the real root of your worries you will, in actuality, only keep them alive. If there wasn't any turmoil to resolve, there wouldn't be any to resist and sometimes, just having a unbiased listener to bounce your worries and frustrations off of, creates an environment that encourages you to truly come to terms with what has been consuming your soul. You are meant to be happy. And who knows? Through therapy, you might just learn something about yourself that you may not have known otherwise.

Skilled professionals are at your disposal. Take the time to find one that works for you. The search should be handled like any other investment you will make in your life: thought out and researched thoroughly. Find a good therapist to talk to, even if it's just for one session. Many health care programs provide their own behavioral health specialists, local nonprofit organizations can help steer you in the right direction or ask your general practitioner for a recommendation. There are so many resources available to you. Find one and release all the frustration you are holding onto, open up that space for something positive, knowing that this is the beginning to the end of your worry.

Your mind is a mysterious masterpiece. You can be brilliant and foolish all in the matter of seconds and create scenarios, for any circumstance, that have the worst possible outcome or best fairy tale ending. What you may seem to have a difficult time doing, however, is actually accepting things for what they are. The basis for life is pretty simple; but your interpretation, of what goes on around you, is the variable that can make your life unmanageable and your relationships with others so complex.

Stop worrying about situations that are out of your control! You cannot make anyone love you; they either do or they don't. You can't expect everyone to think exactly like you; they either will or they won't. Life happens regardless of how much you try to control it. Hardship may befall you, plans might change, wrenches in the system could be thrown from a million directions but life will continue to go on. Learn to accept uncertainty for what it is: uncertain. Then decide how you are going to act upon it. You must take action to create any kind of change in your life, but staying silent and agonizing over what you can, or cannot, do only weighs down your body, mind and spirit and leaves you in the exact same spot: miserable. You might not be able to instantly change the circumstances of your life but you most certainly can change your state of mind. It takes work but it is possible!

Worrying about things you cannot control is a choice. Instead, choose to find *positive* ways you can respond to situations that are out of your control. Learn to recognize what you are upset about and find a healthy solution to resolving your sadness, tension or anxiety.

Exercise, help someone in need, write, make music, paint, pray, do some yard work, try therapy, meditate, your possibilities are endless! Find an outlet and then finally allow yourself to acknowledge, heal and let go of your worry. Like a dog chasing it's tail, brooding keeps you spinning in the same unproductive circles, leaving you dizzy and exhausted. If you are unwilling to confront what troubles you, then you have consciously chosen to live in a miserable world of unease and worry. Life "is what it is." Choose to make your "is" good.

So many of us worry about the future. Are we going to be OK? Is our family going to be alright? What if this happens? What if this doesn't happen? My life will be better when...well, guess what? The future hasn't happened. You are choosing to worry about issues that don't even exist! I am not suggesting to throw caution to the wind, but create thoughts that make you excited about your future, not worried.

No one can accurately tell you what the future holds. You can plan for the worst, hope for the best and wish for the most but life will unfold the way it unfolds, regardless of how much you worry about it! Your worry doesn't change circumstance, it doesn't prevent pain and it doesn't ensure happiness. Your <u>choices</u> change circumstance, your courage determines how you handle pain and your consistent actions, based on compassion for yourself and others, is what determines your happiness.

When you find yourself in a worrisome state of mind, force yourself to fill your mind with something else, something positive. <u>Think</u> of the good that is happening around you. <u>Make</u> something good happen around you. Sing a song or read something inspirational, but do what you can to redirect your focus. Let unsubstantiated thoughts, and worry, drift away from your soul and concentrate your energy on something that is real, start with something like forgiveness.

Forgiveness can be one of the most powerful acts of release you will ever experience because animosity and resentment affect only one person: YOU. Worrying about wrongs others may have imposed on you, does nothing to affect another person and does not change the fact the wrong happened. What worry <u>does</u> do is cause your body literal stress and fills your mind with negativity; which, as a result fills your moments, your days and your life with negativity. The only purpose worry serves is keeping you locked in the incident you so desperately want to forget.

Forgive them. Forgive those who have caused you harm or unrest, because your soul does not need to be bogged down for a second longer. Your emotional wounds, that have been festering in your mind and spirit, require time and compassion to heal. In forgiving those who have hurt you, you allow those wounds to start mending, healing from the inside out. Begin to free yourself, from the burden of the past, by releasing any resentment or hurt. Start tenderly applying the ointment of forgiveness to your own wounds, so they can one day become scars and eventually fade.

Keep your attention from replaying any wrong an individual has committed because that wrong is an issue they, themselves, must resolve. It is no longer yours. And the only way to rid yourself of the turmoil from past mistakes, whether they belong to you or someone else, is to make sure the same mistakes don't happen again. You cannot make the wrongs disappear unless you stop recreating them in your mind and through your actions. Commit to being your best self, and be at peace with the simplicity of living a life based on healthy choices and connectedness. Direct your attention to what is good, and what is real, in your life and then, most importantly: *forgive yourself.*

Forgive yourself for mistakes you have made. You have made

them once, or twice or maybe even more than that...but you do not have to repeat them again. You have that choice! Instead of constantly beating yourself up for wrong decisions you have made, and for they way you have treated people in the past, get to the root of your regrets! If they involve someone you have wounded, humbly ask for their forgiveness. If they accept your apology, be grateful! Be at peace and finally put the situation to rest.

If they do not accept your apology: do what you can to rectify the situation, then graciously accept there is nothing more you can do. You cannot *force* anyone to forgive you. You can only attempt to correct the wrongs you have made in you life and believe that, eventually, all will be made right.

In saying you are sorry and asking for forgiveness, be comforted in the fact that you have done what you can, to help someone begin to release any hurt you have imposed on them; hurt that may be impeding them from becoming the whole person they are so capable of becoming.

You are human. You will make a mistake now and then, but the beautiful power you have in either repeating, or learning from, those mistakes is what determines the difference between a great day and one of regret. Be conscious of making healthy choices, in doing so, you will be bringing your worry and agonizing days of torment to an end.

It's easy to get caught up in the misconception that life should run smoothly all of the time: relationships should be bliss, children should be angels, work should be rewarding. And (God forbid) if a disruption takes place stress floods the gates, tension rises and worry creeps into every one of your thoughts. Life isn't always smooth. There has to be balance. There will always be the give and take, the up and down and the positive and negative. You cannot have one without the other. So, on days when things are good embrace them! Don't be afraid to revel in the goodness, and light, that you experience.

Sometimes when things are going your way, you may start to wonder "when is the ball going to drop?" You become weary of "why" good things are happening and brace yourself for an unforeseen upheaval, because you think you don't deserve a full, happy existence. This thought process couldn't be more wrong! **You are meant to be happy!** And having joy in your life does not mean that you will have to eventually pay for it by suffering.

Life happens. And if you respect each moment, whether it is positive or negative, for being a moment that adds depth and substance to your existence you won't have anything to worry about! Enjoy the good days and happy moments; embrace them and be ever grateful. If the next day is a little more challenging, instead of worrying about it, try slowing down. Work through it, and take many deep breaths throughout the day knowing, in due course, that it will get better. You have lived through turmoil and suffered heartache, but you are still standing and have survived.

Any heaviness you feel will eventually lighten, and down times will pass, as long as you continue to move forward. Choose to do things that help make your day simple instead of complicated. Be resourceful and be creative, because a problem always has a solution; it's just the one you haven't thought of yet.

There are those of you who have suffered a cruel and devastating past. Whether you have survived mental, emotional, physical or sexual abuse none of it is justified and none of is excusable. But if you are holding this book in your hands and reading the words on this page there is one thing that is for certain...YOU ARE A SURVIVOR. You were thrown into a pit of literal hell but miraculously came up still breathing. What you have done, to hold on this far, makes you absolutely extraordinary!

You had the inner strength, the love for yourself and the determination to have overcome the hideous depths of despair; a laudable feat in its own right. And the beauty of that amazing strength is that it's *still* inside you. *It never goes away.* It may be buried, or it may be fleeting, but it is *still there*. That very strength is forever a part of your soul.

Start digging it back up! Your strength is what you need to hold onto not the worry and agony. Grasp it, build upon it and use it every day for the rest of your life. As for the sadness, the anger, the pain and the hate those are the burdens you need to own, feel and then finally set free.

Say ENOUGH to the dark clouds of trepidation keeping you shielded from the light of a new beginning. Release the heavy loads you are bearing that continue to hold you down. Be bitter then release the bitterness. Be hurt then release the hurt. Be angry then release the anger, because once you free yourself of the toxic emotion you have kept inside -for far too long- you will then have space in your soul to fill.

When you finally make the decision to rid yourself of festering turmoil, fill up the newly open space in your soul with something sweet, something peaceful and something hopeful. But if you are in an abusive marriage, relationship or work environment GET OUT NOW!!!

There is no justification or excuse for abuse. It is **wrong**, and you should not and do not have to be subjected to it. Deep down, you know you are not suppose to be abused physically, emotionally or mentally. Listen to your inner self telling you that you do not have to take this horribly destructive behavior, regardless of what anyone else has to say. Everything that is telling you to leave is RIGHT. The pain and fear you feel is NOT RIGHT. You _must_ summon all the courage inside you, even if you think there is only one drop remaining, and remove yourself from the damaging relationship you have been exposed to. You will be able to overcome any future hurdles that may be preventing you from leaving, because once you find the strength to leave you will, from that glorious moment on, find the strength to do what is necessary to make you life the best it can be. You _cannot_ stay in an abusive relationship, because the toxic environment will not get better with time; it will only get worse. You _deserve_ a life of peace. Please get help and please GET OUT! Do not wait another second.

You are capable of having a full life, you are suppose to feel at peace and you are meant to be happy. Embrace your strength and accept that a good life is what you want to live; a good life is what you are going to have! Make the decision and don't look back, because your life is too precious and your time here is too short.

Stop worrying about what others are thinking or saying about you. Live an honest life being true to the positive things you believe in and, amazingly, everything else will fall into place. It really will! Worry is a cloak for your spirit, a cap for your mind and a heavy suit of armor for your body. It does not serve a healthy purpose. Life continues to happen whether things are right or wrong, it does not shut down and it does not stop. You don't have to either!

The Prayer of St. Francis

Lord, make me an instrument of your peace,
Where there is hatred, let me sow love;
where there is injury, pardon;
where there is doubt, faith;
where there is despair, hope;
where there is darkness, light;
where there is sadness, joy;

O Divine Master, grant that I may not so much seek
to be consoled as to console;
to be understood as to understand;
to be loved as to love.
For it is in giving that we receive;
it is in pardoning that we are pardoned;
and it is in dying that we are born to eternal life.

"You cannot find peace by avoiding life."
~Virginia Woolf

Chapter 7

The Bitch

definition:

a malicious, unpleasant, selfish person, esp. a woman

7

"I've learned that people will forget what you said,
people will forget what you did,
but people will never forget
how you made them feel."
　　　　　　　　　　　　~Maya Angelou

*W*e know who we are...

    the women who always have something critical to say about any "one" and any "thing." We are never satisfied. Respect for others is not something we practice, because we know everyone else is out to get theirs too and everyone has a price. To us, people fall into one of two categories:

    1) those who have something to offer us
    2) those who don't have something to offer us

and for those who don't, they are simply bodies taking up *our* space. If only everyone could be just like us this world would be a much better place.
    We don't trust anyone enough to confide our truest self. Besides, we are too busy sizing everyone up to care about trusting them anyway. The world is a dark, unstable place where we have no one to count on

but ourselves. "Unconditional" love does not exist (everything in life has conditions) and, as a result, we have chosen to keep our hearts cold and calloused. Being vulnerable is death to us and being open to others requires letting down our walls, something we are not interested in.

Disappointment, anger and frustration have chipped away at our shoulders for years, so it's no wonder we cannot help but be consumed with ourselves and survival. And in the midst of it all, we simply don't have frivolous time to "take care of" our soul:

a beautiful soul, and one that is meant to be open to and shared with others. The time has come to start experiencing what is hidden behind the concrete walls that surround your heart: connectedness, compassion and happiness.

"Bitchiness" is a habit, yes a habit, and one that can be quite challenging to break. As human beings we are wired to connect. It has been proven, time and time again, that the way we communicate with the people in our lives, the dynamics of our relationships and the degree to which we relate to, and care for, others affect our own health and well- being, right down to the way our hormones regulate our hearts and immune systems. Healthy, positive relationships actually promote our biological health while stressful relationships create biological havoc.

When you are happy and healthily feel good, you have a natural inclination to nurture your well-being (and the well-being of those you care about) but when you are miserable on the inside or, in a constant state of unease, your well-being adversely suffers.

In an unhappy state, your connection to other people becomes one fueled by negativity, and negative connections inevitably lead to one conclusion: unhappiness. Unhappiness in your relationships, your self-worth, your perception of this world and all of the people in it. Instead of seeing what is good in others, you automatically search for, and hone in to, what is bad. Everything and everyone becomes a problem and all too often, the common denominator shared by unhappy women is "bitchiness."

Starting at a very early age, you see it and hear it everywhere. Unhappy women connecting through complaining, nagging, criticizing, judging, jealously, anger and loathing of all that is not like them. But amazingly, no woman is just "born" bitchy, we become that way. Our pettiness and criticisms of each other are not inherent qualities of being female. The need to *communicate* may be an inherent quality, but each unkind word you say, each attitude you give, each judgment you pass are decisions *you* make.

The way you participate in your relationships spreads either negativity or positivity and, in doing so, you ask the world to negatively or positively reciprocate. So what would happen if you decided to approach things differently? For just one day instead of choosing to behave and speak negatively, what if you chose to behave and speak positively? Try this for *one day* and see what happens:

1) Every time you start to THINK a negative thought, force yourself to focus on something positive instead

2) Every time you are going to yell or scream at someone, take a deep breath, literally count to five (aloud) and speak without raising the volume of your voice

3) Expect the *best* in the people you interact with, not the worst

4) When you engage in conversation with another women, let it surround an encouraging topic, not anything destructive, condemning or demeaning

5) If you start to CRITICIZE yourself, or anyone else, STOP! Actually tell yourself to stop. And if you cannot find something good to say, refer to the old adage...
"DON'T SAY ANYTHING AT ALL!"

Make it a daily goal to stop speaking negatively about people, because a life that has a sense of purpose is not centered around trite conversation. If you are actually filling your life with something substantial, you won't have much time to waste on petty gossip.

However, if you *do* sincerely have a problem with someone, talk directly to *them* about it and make the conversation constructive (refer to Chapter 4), but stop discussing people who are not around to defend themselves. This kind of conversation can be devastating. When you engage in demoralizing or demeaning conversation about anyone, you are creating negative words through your negative thoughts. You spread negativity and, as a result, negativity will be what you continue to experience.

You deserve to have a life that is full, not empty, and being a catalyst for negativity only creates a distinct barrier around you that rebounds real connectedness and creates destruction and havoc. Why would you choose to contribute to the world this way? You may have been influenced by a need, and desire, for creating unease and the madness could be what you find comfort in, but it is not an inevitable way of life. *You do not have to continue to live this way.*

What kind of conversation do you choose to engage in? Do you speak about topics that interest you, people who move you or issues that concern you? Are your conversations geared toward ideas that really stimulate your mind? Or do you seem to always end up talking about someone else? Make your conversations useful. Make each word you say be one of meaning, not malice, and then start to notice how you feel.

Disagreements can be challenging but they are also a natural part of life. We all have a unique perspective of our miraculous world and, we won't always see eye to eye. But just because you disagree with someone does not mean the discussion must turn into a heated battle. If you find yourself "fighting" with others the majority of the time instead of "healthfully discussing", it is time to address your personal unresolved tension. It is this very tension, and personal frustration, that ultimately creates the reason for a fight not necessarily differing viewpoints. The tension is like smoldering magma; it has to surface somewhere.

Being an emotional time-bomb waiting to explode is not a productive, nor healthy, way to engage in relationships. You must address the tension inside you and find a healthy way to resolve it.

Imagine what it feels like to be at ease with those in your life. Instead of waiting for them to say (or do) something that will make you angry to the point of a personal explosion, imagine regularly residing in "calm mode" instead of always rearing back in "attack mode." Think of the energy you would have! Think of the sleep you would get! Think of the joy you would experience instead of the hate. You can learn how to simplify your life or you can make it more difficult; it's up to you.

A healthy first step, toward a life of simplicity, would be to reacquaint your soul to experiencing satisfaction through what is **_good_** and what is **calm**, not what is hostile, angry or destructive. Conserve your energy and expend it on what is productive, constructive and healthy. Make the battles you engage in be out of necessity not out of routine.

It is virtually impossible for a woman who is secure, calm and happy to be nasty to anyone, because a content spirit does not try to tear another soul to pieces. Tumultuous relationships indicate tumultuous souls, so start to notice your initial reaction to people. The way you judge and view others is a direct reflection of the the way you view yourself, and if you are sincerely happy with who you are (flaws and all) seeing the good in others will be natural; searching for what is "bad" won't even be a concern for you.

Get to the root of why you really think you despise someone. Are you jealous? Are you threatened? Were they distrustful? Any energy you are using to hate someone is wasted energy. There is a *definite* reason why you feel animosity, jealousy, anger, rage or resentment toward someone. You have to get to the root of your emotion because, more than likely, it results from an unresolved issue within yourself. Learn to have compassion for those people you feel negatively about.

The definition of jealousy is "feeling or showing envy of someone or their achievements and advantages." When you experience this emotion, honestly ask yourself "what is causing me to feel this way?" "What am I jealous of?" Usually, it is because you want something that someone else has: confidence, accolades, looks, health, intelligence, family life, wealth. Jealousy is a good indication that you, consciously or subconsciously, feel you are lacking in some way, shape or form. How wonderful it is that you are the *only* one who can change your achievements, your confidence and your self-worth.

So, if you start to feel a twinge of jealousy, remember to embrace the qualities *you* have and all *you have to give*. You don't have to compare yourself to everyone else but, instead, take a moment to think about who you are and what special qualities make you, uniquely, *you*.

Just because someone may embody the personal characteristics or a particular way of being that you wish to have, does not mean you have to *envy* them. Let these people *inspire* you. Transform your envy and jealously into admiration. Then make a plan, and decide exactly *how* you are going to healthily accomplish your goals to attain what you desire.

Use your energy to find resources that will aid you in determining a path that leads to the healthy place you wish to reside. If other women seem to already be there, learn from them and open up to them. Hating them will provide you with nothing but resentment and waste the energy you could be directing toward self improvement. You will either make changes to achieve your goals or you won't. It is your choice.

Feeling threatened, not in a violent manner but in an envious manner, is another good indicator of needing to look inward at your own insecurities. When you are confident in who you are, and what you have to offer this world, nothing will shake you. Sure, we all have moments of self-doubt but they should be fleeting not permanent. If you do experience a pang of concern about the security of your job, a relationship or anything that offers you a sense of stability, take a step back and reevaluate your involvement. Are you doing what you can? Is your heart in it? Focus on giving your best self to your endeavors and you will have no reason to feel threatened by anyone.

All you can give is your best and if you are doing just that, life will unfold the way it is intended. You cannot give any more, you cannot be anymore and you cannot create anymore. Reside in your healthy, true self! You are you, and there is <u>nothing</u> in this world that can threaten that.

There comes a point in all of our lives, where we have to say good-bye to the people who continuously suck the life out of us. Even the brightest light can be diluted by enough darkness, and regardless of your strength or your convictions, negative people will be a catalyst to your misery. Take a look at the kind of women you chose to spend time with. Outside of obligation, who are you surrounded by? Motivated women? Compassionate women? Angry women? Any women? Who you choose to surround yourself with not only *reflects* who you are but also *affects* who you are. Happy women connect through mutual respect and openness. "Bitchy" women connect through their ability to find fault in others and cynicism.

Some of us have friends in our lives we have know for ages. Take a moment to reflect on what brought you together and what keeps you together. What commonalities do you share? Observe the activities you engage in when you spend time together. Are they healthy? Are they positive? If they are, nurture these relationships and be the kind of friend you would want to have. Cherish each friendship for the bond you have created and find ways to make it even better, but if your relationship is not rooted in what is healthy, you have two choices:

1) work on recreating a friendship that cultivates goodness in what you do together, your conversations and your motivation for spending time with one another

2) distance yourself

for the sake of your well-being, for the sake of your progress and for the sake of your life. It is crucial you surround yourself with those who are striving to live a life full of goodness, because you cannot swim in a cesspool and come out smelling like roses. You just simply can't.

Family members cannot be dropped. If your family is sprinkled with malicious, unpleasant women this is your opportunity to spark a change in the family dynamic (one everyone will be grateful for). Your emotional state affects EVERYONE and being a part of a family means being a responsible component of connectedness.

There is always a vast array of personalities, talents, strengths and weaknesses within a family. Again, we are extraordinary beings but our lives are about more than just us, and a healthy family unit is a place where your soul can be nourished by some of the deepest, most pure love you will ever experience. On the other hand, within an unhealthy family unit you will experience forces that can be some of the most devastating and destructive to your soul and progress, and as matriarchs to our families, it is our responsibility to contribute to the former not the latter.

The way you behave toward, and interact, with the women in your family has an effect on *everyone*. You have the capability to positively influence and change the energy surrounding your immediate and extended family, by being an example of what is good and by contributing through compassion and strength.

Just imagine what our families would be like, if the women were happy in their own right and helpful, and open, to each other! Where honest communication and mutual respect were natural components of our relationships. Imagine how the remaining family members would be affected. Again, you have the capability to choose what you create.

BE NICE! Your words are your thoughts. Take a moment to examine what your mind is filled with and honestly observe the way you treat those closest to you. Are you speaking kindly to them?

Name calling and derogatory remarks are neon signs reflecting the way you feel about you, not necessarily anyone else. Every time you curse someone, every time you berate someone you are expressing some kind of internal unrest.

Healthy spirits do not try to tear others down. So, if you find yourself saying hurtful things to people, stop and figure out where the hurt is actually coming from. Get to the root of your unhappiness and refrain from taking it out on other people, because the amount of respect you give to others determines the amount of respect you would like to receive. Resolve your inner turmoil and make your thoughts worth sharing; speak words others want to repeat not forget.

Take initiative! The time has come to derail your sense of entitlement because the only person who owes you anything is *you*. The irony in expecting others to give you what you want is that if you actually did something for yourself, to get what you want, others would be more willing to give to you. To have a life filled with achievement, you must actively achieve and the only reward you <u>will</u> gain from sitting on your behind is a very sore behind.

Start with simple choices and take a moment to honestly ask yourself "what do I *really* want out of life?" Do you want inner peace, good health, stable finances, strong relationships, a different career, deep spirituality or just a good night's sleep? What one thing can you focus on today to bring positive change into your life? Take the time, and space, to plan a strategy. Grab a piece of paper or open your laptop, sit down and create a plan about how you are going to make the changes happen, because if your life has consisted of doing x, y and z and the final results don't equate to happiness, it is time to change the variables to a, b and c.

Take pride in the fact you have the ability to do something for yourself! Because if you have the capability to think about what you want, you have the ability to create what you want. Nothing in life comes easy; you must be willing to expend your time, and energy, in order to reap the benefits you want out of life. If you are not willing to work for what you desire, don't expect to get it and be content with your decision. There is no use in complaining nor feeling slighted about not getting what you "deserve" in your lifetime, if you aren't willing to make the changes of your own accord.

Life is meant to be lived and accepting, and working through, challenge is what builds your character. Examine the lives of the leaders you admire, and notice how none of them rose to where they are out of charity. They are people of action! They got off of their rumps and pursued their passion. That very strength is in you too!

Unfortunately, having strong personality traits may lead you to believe that other people perceive you as being a "bitch", so you fall into the trap of thinking you have to manifest and uphold that "role." You think that if you aren't critical, other's won't respond to you; if you aren't harsh they will think you're soft and if you aren't nasty you will not be respected. It's what they expect from you, so it's what you must continue to give. This couldn't be further from the truth.

Being objective and being condemnatory are two *completely* different actions. Just as being strong-willed and being a "bitch" are two *completely* different actions. You can still have an opinion. You can still be determined. You can still be assertive and in control of yourself without being a woman who is malicious or unpleasant. What we are addressing here is the unhappiness, the vindictiveness and the having to find fault in others that constitute the 'bitch' role that the women of this chapter often become consumed by. Living this way isn't as necessary as you think it is.

The next time you are confronted with a situation where you could react maliciously, nastily or vindictively remind yourself of this...we are all here just trying to survive the best way we know how. We all came into this world the same way and we're all going out the same way. If you choose to make this life pleasant for yourself and others, that is exactly what your life will end up being. We are human and all of our needs are really quite basic. We need to eat, drink and breathe; we need our health and safety; we need intimacy, family and friends and lastly some kind of positive self-esteem.

We *all* need the *exact same things* to survive and thrive! We each had to rise out of bed this morning (whether we were rested or not), grab something to eat and begin our day, to differing degrees we have all felt joy and frustration; each of us have laughed and cried and have stolen moments, here and there, to wonder how we could make our life a little bit better than it is right now. So, when you come in contact with another woman, whether it's an acquaintance or stranger, whether she's younger or older, larger or smaller, lighter or darker, richer or poorer whoever she is, instead of looking her up and down, making a quick judgment of her and then turning away, make eye contact with her and smile. Yes, SMILE! Simple acts of kindness can go a loooong way, for you and the other person.

Try it and see what happens, because if we can all strive to remember how much we have in common and offer kindness to each other instead of hurt, our positivity will begin to feed off of itself. The concept is simple and it makes sense; if you don't believe it just notice how negativity spreads like wildfire. It's the exact same process, just a different ingredient.

Be good to yourself, be gentle and be kind and as a result, you will be all of those things to others. Being negative is not healthy, it not only wears you thin and fills you with toxic emotion, but it will also eventually break your spirit. If you choose to continue to be negative, you are consciously choosing a life of misery. It is that simple. When you are sincere in your actions, and beliefs, you add light to the conversations you engage in, your presence is welcomed and you *feel* good. And inherently

you are suppose to feel good.

Start by being a role model to the young women of our world. They have become so consumed with two aspects of their lives that can change in the blink of an eye: the way they look and what they own. Young girls are learning, at a very early age, what it means to be sensual and sexual. They are inaccurately thinking that monetary value means substance and the more they fit in with the superficial, the further they will get ahead in life.

It is your responsibility to redirect their attention. You have to teach them -first and foremost- the importance of being mentally, physically and spiritually healthy. That it's not what *they look like* or what *they have* that defines them but, more importantly, it's what *they stand for* and how they *treat other people.*

You must teach them to nurture their health and exude happiness. Nurture their minds and develop intelligence. Nurture their talents and develop passion, to stand up straight, keep their chins up and develop confidence. These are the qualities you need to cater to in young women! You must give them opportunities to discover their own strengths and weaknesses. Support them in healthy endeavors, because once they have established a solid belief in who they are on the inside, it won't be as easy for them to compromise who they are on the outside.

We all can, and should, look and feel *our* best. But in setting an example of how to live a happy life we must emphasize what it means to be healthy and the importance of cultivating the intangibles: intelligence, humor, inquisitiveness, strength, motivation, self-acceptance, responsibility and compassion. Qualities that create whole, connected women and do not fade with time but become even brighter and more magnificent. This is how we can ensure a lineage of women who will continue to make a positive impact on the world that surrounds us.

"You must be the change you want to see in the world."

~Mahatma Gandhi

Chapter 8

The One-Upper

8

"Pride is concerned with who is right.
Humility is concerned with what is right."
~ Ezra Taft Benson

*W*e know who we are...

the women who cannot tolerate anyone being more intelligent, more accomplished, more attractive or more together than us. Within every conversation, we are always quick to add our two cents, about what we have done, where we have been and where we are going. We are the Ultimate Alpha females. We are uncomfortable if any woman begins to outshine us, and it is then we move in for the kill. It is absolutely essential for us to be on top, at all times: most admired by others, most respected by others and most noticed by others. We have to be the best because if we are not, we may give someone else the opportunity to out do us.

Our personal mantra is simple "Control, Control, Control," every minute, every conversation, every schedule and everybody. There is never a moment where our mind is at rest because (God forbid) we might miss something. Our stress level is usually in overdrive and our energy is expended on making sure everything is perfect: all of the time. Other women *always* pose a challenge. We have to constantly be on our "A" game because we can never appear faulty, unorganized or fragile. Even when others are oblivious to the raging competition going on inside our heads, we are keeping score. We have so much to keep track of that we have lost sight of any beauty in those we feel threatened by and being constantly preoccupied with overprotecting our status has left us with an overprotected heart.

You have tragically forgotten that every person is worthwhile and has something unique to offer this world, even if they are not perfect. Including you.

We all have a story to tell and without our personal experiences we would be left without individuality. Individuality is what creates our uniqueness and is a part of what makes us all so beautiful. Our life experiences shape our personalities, create a template for living and teach us lessons we either choose to learn or repeat. So, it is necessary to share our histories with each other in order to create deeper connections and strengthen intimate bonds.

However, when you become consumed with making certain that every conversation somehow redirects itself back to your accolades, extensive knowledge, unsurpassed experience, unequivocal wisdom and how much more you have done (and always will be doing) than everyone else, you are simply saying, "I am so terribly afraid of not measuring up, that I am going to fill our conversation full of *me* to prove to *you* how great *I* really am." Your participation in the conversation is not used to graciously share your life story, listen to or connect with others, it instead becomes a clear reflection of your hidden self-doubt.

The only person you are responsible for being is you! How wonderful it is that you have your own personality, your own mind, your own talents and your own unique look. No one will ever be exactly like you and you will never be exactly like anyone else...YOU ARE YOU!

Why would you choose to try to live up to anything, or anyone, else? In doing so, you are fighting what is naturally already yours. Embrace who you are, and reside in the peacefulness of knowing there is nothing more, nor anyone else, to "be better than". You just simply need to be *you*.

We are not perfect. Human beings are not made that way and we are not intended to be. Attempting to live at a level of "perfection" is purely an effort in vain because being a perfect person is impossible.

The definition of perfect is "being faultless, without flaw or defect in condition or quality." So, if any *thing* is faultless there is no reason for it to change. But people **are meant to change!** You are meant to experience, and learn from, life; to grow and amazingly evolve. If you think you have reached any level of perfection, you have actually reached the exact moment of intellectual and emotional death. You can always strive to be your best but in this lifetime you will never be perfect, and thank goodness for that!

Life is about continuous growth and evolution. Living is about residing in the core of your truest self and being the best version of *you*. So, instead of exerting your energy on comparing how you measure up to someone else, use that energy to focus on your unique qualities and how you can be as physically, mentally and emotionally healthy as possible. Once you simplify the direction of your focus, you will then begin to see the simple beauty inside yourself and that same simple beauty in others.

Think of your life like it's an onion and at the core of the onion is your wonderful, sweet soul. Each layer of the onion represents the experiences you have during your lifetime; depending on your relationships (and what activities you choose to engage in) the growing layers will either become thick or thin, hard or soft, healthy or rotten. If you ignore the importance of addressing and peeling away an unhealthy layer (i.e. dysfunctional relationships, criticism of others) the massiveness of neglected, compounded layers will slowly, but surely, bury the purity that comes from the core of the onion: your soul.

Your soul is the reservoir from where you will find your strength, compassion, acceptance of yourself and others, understanding and passion. Anything, and everything, that is a part of you will rise from your soul and without great care taken in keeping it free from the debilitating layers of what life may have to offer, this world may become too heavy and your mind, and spirit, may not know how to find peace or clarity. Instead of being open to -and accepting of- others, *competition* will be all you see in other people, not *connection*, and from this sheltered, shallow perspective your focus will always be on one person: you.

Life is not meant to be lived this way. You are meant to connect with others, and in order to do this you must begin to look for, and see, the good in *everyone*.

When you begin to see the goodness in others, you will begin to accept yourself for exactly who *you* are. There will be no need to demand attention, because you will be at ease without it. You won't have to rely on outside validation, because you will feel safe in your own being. Once you are secure in the fact that you are doing all you can to be your best, you won't have the time, nor the desire, to compare yourself to anyone else. All you will need to do is simplify your life, by focusing on the present.

This means understanding that your moments, days, weeks and life might not always be "perfect;" that sometimes you won't know the all of the answers, and that it is healthy (and OK) to say, "I don't know" or "I have never done that." Then, most importantly, start taking some risks and engage in an activity you have never experienced before.

There is great humanness in experiencing the unknown! In doing so, you allow yourself to venture into areas that are outside of your comfort zone (promoting growth!) and when you tread on unexplored ground it is expected you will, at some point, stumble. Stumbling is OK! Because when you do fall (and we all do) you immediately have to find a way to get back up. You don't become any less of a person because you stumble; quite the contrary. You only become stronger and add more depth to your life because when you make a mistake, you are forced to tap into your resilience and create a new path to follow. You are not expected to walk a "perfect path" in this lifetime, just keep walking.

So, relax, take a deep breath and have some no pretense fun. The kind of fun that hasn't been planned out, weighed out or "made sure" to be more fun than the fun other people are having. Your time here is so short; don't take yourself too seriously. By simply being who you are, you give our world another beautiful spirit and body to celebrate! Stop being so hard on yourself because *you* are the very best *you*, there has ever been! Take the enormous pressure of perfection off of your shoulders and let yourself *be*.

Unpredictability will always happen. Flow when you are confronted with adversity and when you are faced with a challenge: give yourself the opportunity to look at alternative options in finding a solution. Do your best, be satisfied with it and surrender to the fight of rigidness and absolutes.

Life happens, and getting worked up because you may have messed up only creates stress on your body, mind and soul; stress that prohibits you from being your true self. You are no less of a person, and you are no less capable, if you make a mistake or take a little time to stop and smell the roses. If you choose to stay locked in your world of having to do, have and create it all, be aware that you are priming yourself for that "one" day when you take a look behind you and wonder where, when and why it was you stopped actually living.

It is important to be, and do, your best in any endeavor, but you cannot reach a state of balance if one aspect of your life takes precedence over all others. In trying to manage work, children, schedules or perfectionism there must be a common ground. That common ground: your healthy well-being.

Nourishing your mind, body and spirit promotes healthiness in all aspects of your existence, but inevitably, one area will suffer if you do not take the time to remember, and experience, what this life is all about in the first place. Healthy personal connections that are rooted in balance and compassion -starting with your *own* self-acceptance- are what fuel contentment and peace.

You have so much beauty ready to burst from inside you by simply being you! But when you force the drive of perfectionism, emotionally, you miss precious moments of simplicity because your hyper focused attention doesn't allow you to naturally observe, and absorb, the sublime nuances of life.

Striving for perfection is like taking a long road trip that only consists of driving at a constant speed of 80 miles per hour, on the same stretch of interstate, making intermittent restroom breaks out of necessity. Your concentration is only on the road in front of you with one destination in mind. Your extreme determination in straining to read each upcoming road sign and constant monitoring of the traffic that is pulling ahead of you, prevents you from taking in the beautiful foliage along the way. Any charming side roads are missed as well as the sunsets and sunrises that could be better observed, sipping a cup of coffee from a roadside cafe.

Once you *finally* reach your destination you will be exhausted and unclear about what you just experienced because your *only* focus was the destination: having to get there first and fastest. Your mind was always one step ahead, consumed by everything but the purpose of the trip.

When striving to be the best in *everything*, instead of simply being the best you, it becomes difficult to be fully present in *any* relationship, moment, thought or action. Start enjoying the ride! Embrace each day as a gift, live each moment in appreciation for what it has to offer and give yourself the opportunity to experience the beauty of what *already* surrounds you. Give your mind, agenda and anxiousness a rest.

Life is ever changing. Be at peace with who you are. Embrace every aspect that uniquely makes you, *you*, even your imperfections, because we all have them and it's OK! Our strengths and weaknesses are what make us human.

Your actions represent your truest self so, instead of having to tell everyone how wonderful you are *do* something wonderful for them! Before you begin telling others about how interesting *your* life is, ask them about *theirs*. Remember: **everyone has a story**. Find out what dreams and fears the people who are dear to you harbor (because we all have some of each) and in doing so, you just might discover you happen to share the same hopes or hang-ups. Give yourself the chance to open up and be vulnerable, because emotion is what makes you human; it let's you feel and, most importantly, it allows you to connect.

Get to the root of why you feel you must prove to others how good you really are. Does it stem from a need for validation and reassurance? Both of which are used to quell the feeling of insecurity.

If so, why are you insecure?

If your actions represent your truest self and convictions, what more reassurance do you need? When you engage in conversations, and relationships, knowing your thoughts, words and deeds honestly reflect your true thoughts and feelings, what more is there to be concerned about? Simplify your life by being honest with others and honest with yourself. In doing so, you will prevent uncertainty, and insecurity, from creeping in and taking over your thought process.

Celebrate women who make a positive impact with their lives and give them an opportunity to let their own light shine. Their successes do not take away from yours! Be happy for *anyone* who achieves a goal or does something great.

If you observe or interact with someone who has personality traits you admire do not hate them for it, *compliment them.* You love receiving a compliment just as other people do. Make it a habit to sincerely compliment someone every single day. It feels so much better to have a heart that is full instead of a mind full of snide remarks and when you feel better, notice how the people around you feel better. It's an intriguing concept! (and it works!)

Breathe, relax and be patient with others. When you place the enormous pressure on your shoulders to be perfect, the pressure is automatically felt by the people who surround you, and just because you choose to walk a tight rope doesn't mean those you interact with have to walk it too. Encourage others to be their best selves, but abstain from placing your expectations of perfection on them. It is a massive load for them to bear that first, they did not ask for and second, is only fuel for resentment.

Encourage others to answer to their inner calling but allow them to live at their own unique pace, because they are not you and you are not them. Your bests will not be the same because you are different people; that's how this beautiful life operates. And the most effective way to encourage greatness is to simply be an example of it. Not by forcing it, not by talking about it and not by criticizing others for achieving it in a different manner than you would. Be it, live it and become your greatest self. That is all you have to focus on. You do not have to consume yourself with being better than anyone, nor is it healthy to judge others in their own pursuit of greatness. Be an example of what is good and watch what magically unfolds.

Now, on to a more sensitive subject that must be addressed when acknowledging self-destructive behavior: having romantic relationships with married men and women. There is nothing right about sabotaging any one else's happiness for, what you think, is the sake of your own. If you find yourself seeking out, dating or sleeping with someone who is married, the time has come to confront your self-worth.

Throughout this book, we continue to address the importance of healthy relationships in order to experience true happiness. Honest, positive personal interactions, accompanied by compassion for yourself and others will be the kind of relationships that are most beneficial to your progress. On the other hand, the kind of deceit and mistrust that accompanies a sexual involvement with someone who has already committed to a relationship (with someone else) will consequently proliferate deceit and mistrust in your own life.

The longer you engage in a particular behavior, the more commonplace it seems and more comfortable it becomes. Time doesn't change the substance of morality, your perception does. Time doesn't change the essence of self-worth, your dignity does. Remember, "what you choose to engage in is what your life becomes" and you are the *only* one who decides what you are worthy of experiencing. You deserve to be healthy! And if you feel it is necessary to be involved in a romantic relationship, you deserve to be a part of one that is rooted in truth and gives you more than the 50% of what you are receiving.

Yes, it takes two to tango, but if someone is married and chooses to cheat on their spouse, let it be with someone other than you. Respect *yourself* enough to refuse to enter into a relationship with someone who is already committed. Respect the *other woman* enough to refuse to be with someone who is already committed her. If you are involved with someone who is unhappy in their existing relationship, it is an issue *they* need to resolve; if they are in the process of *leaving* their spouse, respect them both as people and give them the space (and time) they need to settle their separation or divorce.

Choose to make your life more simple not complicated. Give your beautiful soul a chance to experience a healthy relationship with someone who is willing to fully engage in a relationship with you; not just when it's convenient and not while their divorce is "pending."

Create personal experiences in your life that are positive not negative. You deserve to have a good life, not one shadowed by dishonesty, but you are the only one who can put yourself in the positive situations, and nurturing relationships, that offer you that goodness. YOU ARE THE ONLY ONE WHO DECIDES.

It is so important to treat other women with respect. Remember, everyone has a personal story, and if the notion of having compassion and respect for others, regardless of their success, ethnicity, pedigree or age is completely alien to you, there is deeper aggravation inside you that needs to be uncovered.

The way you participate in, and view, life (whether you are conscious of it or not) creates a "standard" in regard to what you deem acceptable behavior and unacceptable behavior. This is why it it so important to live a life of goodness and health, if goodness and health is what you want to experience.

The concept is like being scooped up from your home in the middle of the night by a gigantic stork, flow to another country half way around the world and dropped into the middle an enormous, foreign city center. Your way of life (i.e. your language, customs, dress, manners, eating habits, hand gestures) may not necessary jibe with the way of life of the peoples and culture you were just dropped into.

In order to survive, you would have to learn the nuances, language, social mores and customs that are already very natural to the people of the city, because it is their daily way of life. They live it, are surrounded by it, see it, hear it, are shaped and molded by it and it has become their standard. Their way of life is second nature to them.

That's how the ideal of perfection works too. If you continue to force it, reinforce it, live it, surround yourself with it, see it, hear it and become shaped and molded by it, it will become second nature for you to expect it from others. And if you strive to live a life based on perpetual perfection, those who exhibit "imperfect" behavior won't live up to your "standards" and will become unacceptable.

We are all worthy of acceptance! And instead of expecting others to live in a bubble of perfection, created by the standards you have set, try *respecting* others for their unique differences, celebrate the qualities that set them apart and learn from the strengths that are developed.

This doesn't mean you have to adhere to another's way of life, but understand, and respect, that we all have differences in our beliefs, the way we speak, parent, dress, worship, teach and live. It's not important that we all act in the same manner, the importance lies in where our actions are rooted; hopefully in goodness and love. Besides, at the end of the day, if you silently observe the people who make up our miraculous world, you will find that we really are all *so much alike.*

There is a beautiful, and very inspirational, poem written by the amazing Maya Angelou entitled "Phenomenal Woman." Read it, savor each word and then take a look around at the phenomenal women you see everywhere, including the one staring back at you from the mirror.

Be good to yourself! There is so much to enjoy in this lifetime, but if you continue to live in a world that is full of agenda, perfection and a constant state of 150% you will forget how to let go in moments of tranquility. You will forget what stillness feels like and what healing calm, and nourishment, it can offer. You will miss the whisperings of your inner most self telling you how beautiful your life really is. Give your soul an opportunity to soak up the serenity that comes from residing in your most balanced, healthy and good enough self.

*"To be yourself in a world that is constantly trying to
make you something else
is the greatest accomplishment."*
~Ralph Waldo Emerson

Chapter 9

The Hypochondriac

9

"Health is a state of complete physical, mental and social well-being, and not merely the absence of disease or infirmity."
~World Health Organization, 1948

*W*e know who we are...

the women who are always sick. We never have enough energy and on those rare days when we start to feel better, our mind clears a little and our body starts to get back on track...BLAM! We end up having a physical setback and wake up the next morning feeling miserable again. Our head and body feel heavy and without exerting any energy to begin with, we are too depleted to exercise. Exhaustion has settled into every one of our joints, muscles and bones.

Our moments are spent looking forward to sleep, or our next dose of medication, because it is then (and only then) that we will feel better. Our moods are determined by which medication we take and depending on the prescription, we develop side-effects that only dissipate with more medication. We are so lost in our physical quandaries that we have forgotten how to find the healing strength that already exists inside us. The large amount of medication we ingest is beginning to dilute our soul. Our body and mind are consumed with so much from the outside, we no longer know how to feel on the inside.

The time is finally here and the time is now, to start relearning how to heal from the inside out.

Yes you are dying and from the moment you took your first breath, you were one breath closer to your last. That's how the concept of being human works. The process is not morbid, it is simply a fact of life. A fact that begins with birth, the most pure act of living, and ends with death, the most final. You, and everyone around you are living on a life continuum. A beautiful cycle that has a distinct start, and finish, and is filled with all kinds of in-betweens. That is why it's so important to understand how precious every moment of your life is and to be able to honestly acknowledge the inevitable.

Does acknowledging death always make it easier to accept? No. The relationships in your life are what make it so meaningful. The connections, love and friendships you develop are what your existence is all about. So, if your perspective on death only focuses on the great physical loss that is experienced, it can be overwhelming, bleak, dark, depressing and absolutely heartbreaking.

Death is a subject that is rarely discussed until the circumstance arises, and even then, because it can be so painful, conversations about our mortality are often avoided. But if you choose to give yourself an opportunity to look upon death from a different perspective, you may also find a little peace and clarity when having to face the realities of grief, loss, pain and uncertainty.

Give yourself a chance to participate in a healthy dialog about death and dying, and honestly confront your fears, anxieties, questions and personal beliefs. What is it that disturbs you the most? Is there anything you can do to make your thoughts easier to process?

The unknown always has a way of creating terrible confusion and doubt. As a human being, you may find yourself wanting to rationalize *everything* that happens in your life; there must always be a justification as to "why" things happen, right? And when you can't cognitively figure it out, instead of accepting the unknown for being "unknown" it can be easy to become consumed with finding an explanation to help you understand the "why" and "how" of life's circumstances, but not everything in your beautiful life has an explanation. And sometimes, in order to continue to move forward with the life *you* have been given, you must be able to willingly surrender.

You cannot fight the certainty of death, and it's OK What you *can* do, is live your life in a manner that will leave you with no regrets. Tell the people you love *how much you love them*, make the *best* out of *every one* of your experiences and relationships; strive to fill the moments and days you *do* have with goodness and wellness, and be an example of what it means to really *live*. Savor the beauty that surrounds you, and be grateful for all you have been given!

Hopefully, in doing so, you will reach a personal understanding that helps you attain some level of acceptance, and inner peace, when faced with the heart-rendering realities of losing someone you love and your own mortality.

Your time here is precious! The people in your life are precious! Your body is *so* precious and for you to be living, at this exact moment, is nothing short of miraculous!

To begin with, think of the people that had to survive in order for you to exist. You have come from a remarkably strong stock just to get here in the first place, from your parents to their parents, to their parents, to their parents, to their parents the list just keeps going!

Your body is the epitome of resilience but it can only sustain years of nutritional depletion, substance abuse, mental anguish, emotional unease and lack of physical activity for so long. You were born with the necessary faculties to survive (or you wouldn't be reading this book right now). It is up to you to decide if you want to make your body stronger or more fragile, active or inactive, healthy or stale but you cannot escape the inevitable. Part of the process of living is dying, so choose to be consumed with the living part; the dying will take care of itself.

On the outside, your body can amazingly manifest issues that are problematic on the inside. But unless you are aware enough, to recognize these manifestations, they can go unnoticed until the symptom becomes an ailment and the aliment becomes a monstrosity; when you are depressed, overwhelmed or anxious, you not only exacerbate the issues, but it also becomes easy to confuse, or disregard, those very indications your body so desperately tries to convey. Make taking care of your body a priority to help prevent yourself from feeling fatigue, out of shape, always on the verge of illness and completely out of touch.

Fatigue and a lack of proper nutrition are perfect fuel for developing symptoms of disease. If you always feel ill and have lost control of your health you have a choice to make:

1) change your behavior
2) continue to live the way you have been living

"I am not disciplined enough." "I don't know where or how to start." "I have never lived healthily to begin with why should I start now." "I simply don't have the time nor energy." Within each of these excuses is a lie. You <u>are</u> disciplined enough, *you just haven't made up your mind that this is something you really want to do.* You may not know where or how to start, *but it is your responsibility to find out.* If you haven't engaged in a healthy lifestyle, *it is up to you to take the first step in beginning a new journey.* You do have the time, *you just choose to use it for something else* and you don't have any energy because *you aren't properly taking care of yourself.*

Getting rest, eating healthfully and exercising regularly are what you need to focus on, right now, because without each of them, you *will* feel drained. Start healing yourself from the inside out. First step: take care of your body.

There is so much irony in the life of a hypochondriac. The minute you start to *think* you are sick a strange phenomenon happens:

1) Your attention is constantly focused on assessing how run down your body is

2) You become aware of any ache or pain that your body is producing.

3) Your immune system starts to stress because you are feeling stress

and lo' and behold you catch a cold! You are what you choose to focus on. If your thoughts are consumed with illness and sickness, guess what your body thinks is happening?

When you start *anything* new it is a learning process. A change in your diet and exercise regimen may seem daunting because you will, literally, have to change your entire methodology regarding personal health. Not necessarily an easy task because you have been eating, thinking and actively approaching life in the same manner for a very, very long time. You have created a pattern (or path) that your body and mind respond to and in order to change the direction of that path, you have to first acknowledge that the road you are currently on, is not leading you to a pleasant destination. Really take a look at what the past years of your life have consisted of in respect to your physical well-being. Evaluate:

1) how you physically feel every day
2) your energy level
3) your required amount of sleep or lack thereof
4) what kind of food you eat
5) habits that do not promote healthiness
   (i.e. tobacco, drugs, caffeine, excess alcohol, excess sugar)
6) what kind of stress you experience from outside forces
7) how you manage that stress
8) do you have an terminal disorder that requires medical attention

Honestly evaluate each aspect of your physical health. If you are not satisfied with the way you feel, or look, then what you have been doing thus far is not working. It is time to try something new! Commit, right now, to eating differently, increasing your physical activity and healthy maintenance. Set an attainable goal (one year is a good start!) and reevaluate your answers, to the above questions, once you have reached your year end date. If you do not feel better once you get there, you can always go back to your old way of living. It is that simple.

Regardless of where you live, your age, your race or marital status, to physically survive, your body needs the same sustenance as everyone else: food, water, movement and rest. So, what kind of food do you choose to fuel your body with, when was the last time you just drank water, how often do you *move* and is rest even part of your daily routine?

As the years go by we start to complain that we don't have enough energy, we are always so tired and we just don't "feel" good. Is it any wonder, after the years of depriving your body of the essential nourishment it needs, that it starts to break down more quickly than was intended?

Make a commitment to yourself. Give yourself one year to change your life. "ONE YEAR!" you might say, "THAT'S A LONG TIME!" Not in the grand scheme of things it isn't. What is one year out of a lifetime? Especially when it means giving yourself the opportunity to make your life better, more fulfilling and happier.

Initially, it will not be easy. Make this thought process a part of your new life: accepting challenges and being excited about them, not afraid. Learn to experience the great satisfaction in conquering fear, surpassing limitation and savoring achievement. Stop looking for the easy way out, because it is the exact direction that will lead you down the road of fruitless results.

Accept the reality having to *work* for what you want, because once you understand this concept life becomes so much clearer. The good you crave becomes attainable because you stop wasting energy on trying to find ways *around* inevitable hurdles.

Focus on the changes you have to make and accept that they will, at first, be difficult. You will be breaking patterns and giving up all you feel secure in; for example, you will be giving up your unhealthy eating habits (including food you "think" makes you feel better), hours of watching television (you "think" makes you happy) or the listless attitude that prevents you from giving your body the exercise it deserves. You are changing your life! That means you must grow, and remember, growth means letting go of the parts of you that are not working and embracing the new way of life that will bring you so much joy!

When you finally decide to honestly give up these destructive, unrewarding habits, you will inevitably feel a sense of withdraw. A sense of wanting, and needing, that very thing you want so badly to give up. *This is only temporary.* You will be going through a dramatic mental, emotional and physical change. You will be, literally, cutting off the supply of what your body has been (for a very long time)dependent on. And just like pain, grief and evolution, with time you will grow stronger and settle into a better place; a place where your body will have the chance to habituate to a healthy lifestyle.

You have an amazingly powerful mind, you must understand that! Once you realize, and accept, how capable your mind is of overcoming any debilitating weakness, when that weakness presents itself you will only have one task to focus on: conquering **a moment**.

When you are faced with a challenge (whether it is eating unhealthy food, smoking a cigarette or negative self-talk) know you *already* have the power inside to redirect your focus, *just for that moment.* Keep it simple. Tune into why you feel vulnerable. Why do you really think you need to succumb to that moment of weakness? Do you want to eat that candy bar just because it's there? Do you want to smoke the cigarette only out of habit?

Once you acknowledge the reason for wanting what you know is detrimental to your well-being, once you accept that there is a deeper reason pressing you, you then have the incredible opportunity to **reject** it! *It is just a **moment** in your life,* and it takes only *one* choice to create a moment of celebration in defeating that which has controlled you for so long. Prepare yourself for these moments. You can reject the longing to satisfy your weakness with what is unhealthy! You can do this!

Instead of craving the very substances that cause your body distress, your body will begin to want what is healthy. Instead of longing for hours on the couch, your body will miss the days where it can't exert energy. You will start to form new habits. Healthy habits. Habits that encourage healthiness and physically make you your best self; not a body of lethargy and depression.

When you feel good physically, your emotional and mental state are positively influenced as well. Exercise improves what scientists call "executive function": the set of abilities that allows you to select behavior that's appropriate to the situation, inhibit inappropriate behavior and focus on the job at hand, in spite of distractions. Exercise also increases the number of connections between neurons in the region of the brain important for memory, therefore aiding in reducing the risk of disorders, like dementia, late in life. The benefits of exercise are not just limited to maintaining a healthy physique; it actually keeps your brain healthy, too.

Exercise! Even if it is a simple walk. Let the blood flow through your body the way it was intended because your body was built to move! Give yourself 30 minutes; that's all you need. The same amount of time it takes to watch your favorite sitcom. Try it! Stop staring at your walking shoes and STRAP THEM ON! Don't let the thought of exercise overwhelm you because it's a privilege, it does not have to be a torture test. You can engage in *any* type of physical activity: walking, dancing, running, pilates, tai chi, yoga, rollerblading, tennis, cycling, racket ball, basketball, volleyball, golf ANYTHING!

Find an activity you might enjoy and give yourself the time to learn how to enjoy it; because, at some point, you have to be willing to change your routine. You must get over the fear of doing something unfamiliar. Life is about change, and it is about making yourself the very best you! If what you have been doing, thus far, isn't working, it is time to find an alternative. You have nothing to lose (except maybe a few pounds) and everything positive to gain.

Your body was meant to move! Don't let the thought of exercise overwhelm you; instead, take a walk and give your body the exercise it craves, the movement and fresh air it needs. Make a choice to do something physical at least three days a week. Find a buddy to walk with or use your quite walk time for meditation, but start by taking it one day at a time and really listen to your body. Care about yourself enough to get off of the couch, away from the television and off of the computer.

While you are exercising, think about how much good you are doing for yourself. Instead of thinking about how miserable you are while working up a sweat, start thinking about (and saying) how grateful you are to have limbs that work! You have muscles that are gaining strength! You have a miraculous body that can move, run, walk, dance, jump, ride and swim. You are amazing! And with every step you take, think about how you are being energized. Actually say to yourself, "my body is amazing! The way it moves, the energy I create! I am grateful I have the ability to move!"

Change your behavior, visualize and vocalize your adjustment to an active lifestyle and before you know it, you will be experiencing significant changes. It *really* works!

You deserve to feel good! Your body deserves to feel good and if the routine you already have is working, improve upon it! Fine tune your regimen and make it better. You owe it to yourself to physically feel as good as possible, because you only come around this way once. So, go out into this world and make your good, healthy life happen!

Start becoming aware of the fuel you are giving your body to run off of. What you choose to put into your body has a major impact on how you physically feel, from the amount of energy used for digestion to the amount of toxins your body works so hard to expel. Care enough about your well-being to take the time to put the right kind of fuel into your system.

It is not coincidental that eating junk makes you feel like junk. Even though it may seem "easier", or more convenient, to pop a frozen entree into the microwave or pick up the fast food or take out, really take the time to be conscious about what food you choose to eat. Again, *change your long term behavior* by changing the habits you have been catering to for the majority of your life.

Pay attention to what "triggers" your unhealthy habits and then prepare yourself to respond in a different manner. It will take some determination, and patience, to break your body from wanting what it has grown accustomed to, but you *can* do it! Make this change happen one moment at a time; it won't miraculously fall into place overnight but the process *will* eventually become a lot easier! You can do this!

Start to experience different methods of preparing and enjoying your food, *fresh food, healthy food*.

Your taste buds are meant to taste! Try new kinds of food and rely on your *own* opinion to determine what tastes good. Find a culinary club to join or start your own "healthy eating" dinner group. Learn a new approach to preparing different kinds of food; for example, there is a fabulous nonprofit, eco-gastronomic member-supported organization called, "Slow Food", that was founded in 1989 to counteract fast food and fast life. It's a very interesting concept that you should take the time to investigate. Just try it.

Remember, you are the *only* one who decides what fuel goes into your body and you are the last judge to determine if you put the piece of cake, or apple, into your mouth. Open yourself up to new possibilities when it comes to choosing your body's fuel supply.

For one year try changing your eating habits! Sure the apple may not be as satisfying at first, it is not what you are use to, but after weeks of turning to a natural snack, instead of a processed snack, your body will begin to change and crave what is healthful, but first, you have to make a conscious decision to honor your commitment. After a year, it will be your choice to continue on this new path or to go back to your old way of living. Just try it and see what happens!

The next time you are at the grocery store, notice the kind of goods that fill your basket. How many vegetables are your taking home? What about fruit? Are you loaded down with soda or fresh juices? You have been a creature of habit for so many years now. Give yourself just one year out of this lifetime and approach your grocery routine differently, because ultimately it will change your life.

Whether you realize it or not, you probably enter the grocery store through the same entrance and head to the same section every time you go shopping. There are probably sections of the store, or market, that you don't even know exist! So, to begin taking a new approach to your eating habits, start by going through the aisles in an opposite direction than you normally would. Just try it! Force yourself to look at different areas of the market and look for new kinds of food, or products, that are healthier versions of what you are eating right now.

Use the numerous resources available to you by going online for new recipes or picking up a recipe book at a book store. Talk to other women about dishes they like to prepare and tips on how to make healthier meals. Change has to start *somewhere*, and if your eating habits (and concept of nutrition) haven't put you, physically, where you want to be, then DO SOMETHING ELSE. Reprogramming your habits might not be easy, but it will certainly be worth it! Take your new approach one meal at a time.

Think about the eating habits of the generations that have lived before us. Low-carb and no trans-fat did not determine if one was going to eat or not. People ate to sustain life, not to the point of gluttony. We have let ourselves become so busy and over scheduled that we have lost site of the importance of eating healthfully. And when your diet suffers, your health suffers and when your health suffers, *everything* that is a part of your life suffers.

If each day you absolutely, positively, under no circumstance cannot create the time to prepare a healthy meal for yourself, or as a family, then at the *very least* set aside **one** day of the week to do so. Saturday? How about Sunday? You must dedicate **one** day of the week to start making the time to prepare a fresh meal where you can sit down, without the television blaring, with friends and/or family and enjoy a healthy, satisfying meal together.

There is an abundance of good that comes from this. Not just the nutritional benefits but the emotional, and mental, benefits as well. Time set aside to eat a healthy meal together promotes: conversation, an opportunity to spend time with those close to you and moments dedicated to taking care of your well-being. Something that is desperately needed in each of our lives.

The opportunity to seize a life of balance is already within you; the choices you make are all that keep you from obtaining that balance.

Take care of the one body you have been given, and nurture the amazing physical vessel that houses your beautiful soul. You are the only one who determines exactly how it will be done and to what degree you sustain your health, or destroy it. Be good to yourself and take care of your body because, as a result, it will respond by nourishing your mind and spirit.

The manner in which you feed your body, mind and soul creates a constant cycle that is running smoothly or with great strain. You decide if it's the former or the latter.

"No problem can be solved from the same level of consciousness that created it."

~Albert Einstein

Chapter 10

The Happy One

10

"I believe that the very purpose of life is to be happy. From the very core of our being, we desire contentment. In my own limited experience I have found that the more we care for the happiness of others, the greater is our own sense of well-being. Cultivating a close, warmhearted feeling for others automatically puts the mind at ease. It helps remove whatever fears or insecurities we may have and gives us the strength to cope with any obstacles we encounter. It is the principal source of success in life. Since we are not solely material creatures, it is a mistake to place all our hopes for happiness on external development alone. The key is to develop inner peace."

~His Holiness the Dalai Lama

*W*e know who you are...

the woman who can find the positive in any situation and see the goodness in everyone you meet. You are comfortable in your own skin and excited about your place in this world. Your presence is one of strength, motivation and inspiration and you believe everyone has a unique purpose. The patience and compassion you have for those who need it most, is an attribute most of us have yet to understand.

You encourage dreams, are honest in your opinions and steadfast in you convictions. We love and admire you, and have the utmost respect for who you are. You humbly remind us that the beauty we see in you, we all have inside our own selves, and propel us to make that beauty, surpass any reservation we may have about our purpose. You build us up without having to break us down. Our differences you acknowledge and accept; you give of yourself without losing the essence of your own individuality.

You bring women together, in a world where it is so easy to tear each other apart. You are forgiving, you are real and you are happy.

We are all meant to be happy! There is so much good to be experienced in this lifetime. If you find it difficult to be at peace, it is time to dig to the root of your unsettledness and make a commitment to fix what has been broken. You must address your misery, frustration and sadness because your time here is much too precious. Be honest about what keeps you from feeling happy about your life, because it is only then, you can start resolving the turmoil that keeps you from living your fullest existence. Always take the time to ask yourself "What kind of life am I choosing to live?" One filled with catastrophe and unease or one filled with joy and contentment?

Your happiness comes from *within*. When you depend on something else (or someone else) to make you happy, you abandon any control over maintaining your own emotional balance. Each moment you spend waiting for an external "something" to bring you happiness is a moment that has passed in vain. Instead, choose to *create* your joy.

Take stock of how you feel when you spend time alone. It is a wonderful way to calibrate how your inner self is managing. Do you feel uncomfortable? Nervous? Sad? Happy? A healthy spirit is not afraid of itself, nor does it always need someone else there to validate that is alive and well. An amazingly content feeling comes from being able to spend time alone and still feel complete.

Unfortunately, we live in a world where finding a moment of quite solitude can seem virtually impossible, but it is imperative that you create "alone" time in your life to ensure the stability of your well-being. This doesn't mean stealing away for an entire weekend (although it wouldn't be a bad idea) or that you *have* to attend some kind of personal retreat (but if you can, *fantastic!*). What it does mean, is to find a quiet space (whether it's ten to thirty minutes before you hop into the shower in the morning, or ten to thirty minutes before you go to bed at night) to *be still*.

You must be comfortable with spending time by yourself. Be secure, and confident, in knowing that your spirit is strong enough to thrive on it's own and that it is *enhanced* by the relationships that are created in your life, not solely dependent upon them.

Develop an environment of good through the words you speak, the literature you read, the food you eat and the people you who surround you. Choose to make your experiences positive and originate from what is right, honest and pure by being an example of what you believe in, and by treating others the way you would like to be treated. Choose to spend time with people who, not only, exude positivity but also challenge you to be better and *treasure them for it.*

Encourage others to strive toward achieving the goals they set for themselves. Great joy is experienced when you share a dream with someone and they respond by saying, "GO FOR IT!" Be that kind of support to others. When you are happy within your own self, it is natural to be happy for other people and want to see them succeed.

You can motivate others through your actions and set an influential example, by simply being the real you. Remember, within each instance of interacting with someone you are making a difference, so take the time to observe what kind of difference you are making.

Any negative thought that enters your mind, can be turned into a positive one. An undesirable situation you encounter may end up being a helpful lesson learned; a relationship that seems unsalvageable could very well teach you to find forgiveness and inner strength. You always have a choice in the way you perceive, contribute and respond to *any* situation.

Take notice of those women around you who always seem to be happy; one of the most common characteristics they share is charity. Whether it is within their immediate family, a neighborhood, an organization or a nation, individuals at peace are helpful and open to others. Make a commitment to offer a hand to someone in need and observe how simple things like a smile, a wave or just a small act of kindness can transform a moment, which transforms a life: the life of the person you are helping *and* your very own.

There are numerous organizations that have been founded to help those in need. Join one! Find where your passion lies. Is it helping children, single parents, the environment, people with disabilities, veterans, third world countries, people who have heart disease, cancer, AIDS or others diseases and disorders? Maybe you'd like to volunteer for the national park service, a museum, tutor college students, help in the local school system, within your church or maybe just help your *own family*. Your options are limitless! Make a goal to become involved with something that will positively impact the life of someone in need.

Attempt to leave each situation better than you found it, through your words or actions, and engage in what brings about positivity. You can change your life; the process is simple. Choose to embrace what is good, choose to let go of what is bad: emotionally, physically, mentally and spiritually. In doing so, your example will stimulate the good in others and not only will you be *creating* a happy existence for yourself, you will also be an important part of sustaining a greater existence for those around you. It will happen!

Tell the people you love in your life, how much you really love them, and resolve the abrasive relationships that haunt you. Make your wrongs right. Embrace the goodness that surrounds you and the goodness that resides from deep within. You are an extraordinary woman!

Choose to let go of what keeps your soul dim because inside, you have all that is needed to create harmony within your mind, body, soul and relationships. From this moment forward, give yourself the opportunity to live a life that is full and make an impact with your time here.

You have the power within you to be a pillar of strength and connectedness. You have the ability to change the way you view yourself and those who surround you, and you are capable of improving your life one choice at a time.

Choose to create contentment and you will easily pass it on to others. You have the opportunity to influence any situation for the better; choose to be hope, and inspiration, to other women and make your presence positive. Be excited in knowing you are making a noble change and embrace those who encourage greatness, who inspire and always persevere.

With each day that passes, remind yourself of *how miraculous you really are*. You have an unbelievably strong mind, a resilient body and a beautiful soul. Take tender care of each of them and be good to yourself, because you deserve to be happy! There is no need to live up to an unattainable ideal of perfection. You are **you**! With a uniqueness no one else will ever possess! Reside in a life of healthiness, and simplicity, by making your thoughts, words and deeds reflect your truest self. Choose to enhance the goodness in your life, and become an integral part of this positive change that will transform your relationships and help create connectedness among the extraordinary women of our world. You will feel the transformation as it starts to take form, and you will not be able to stop it. You won't want to, and your beautiful spirit won't let you.

The Choice Is Yours.

DO IT ANYWAY

People are often unreasonable, illogical, and self-centered;
forgive them anyway.
If you are kind, people may accuse you of selfish, ulterior motives;
be kind anyway.
If you are successful, you will win some false friends and some true enemies:
succeed anyway.
If you are honest and frank, people may cheat you;
be honest and frank anyway.
What you spend years building, someone could destroy overnight;
build anyway.
If you find serenity and happiness, they may be jealous;
be happy anyway.
The good you do today, people will often forget tomorrow;
do good anyway.
Give the world the best you have, and it may never be enough;
give the world the best you've got anyway.
You see, in the final analysis, it is between you and God;
it was never between you and them anyway.

~Mother Teresa

REFERENCE

[1] WHO "What is Depression?," <u>World Health Organization 2008, http://www.who.int/mental_health/management/depression/definition ed.</u>

www.ingramcontent.com/pod-product-compliance
Lightning Source LLC
LaVergne TN
LVHW011421080426
835512LV00005B/191